60

Sexy Spells of

Seduction

All you need to bewitch your ideal love

60 Sexy Spells of Seduction

All you need to bewitch your ideal love

GILLY SERGIEV

Thorsons

Thorsons
An Imprint of HarperCollins*Publishers*
77–85 Fulham Palace Road
Hammersmith
London W6 8JB

The Thorsons website address is: www.thorsons.com

and *Thorsons* are trademarks of HarperCollins*Publishers* Ltd

Published by Thorsons 2001

10 9 8 7 6 5 4 3 2 1

© Gilly Sergiev 2001

Gilly Sergiev asserts the moral right to be identified as the author of this work

A catalogue record for this book is available from the British Library

HB ISBN 0 00 713027 9
PB ISBN 0 00 713736 2

Printed and bound in Great Britain by Martins The Printers, Berwick upon Tweed

Dedication

To:

Everyone who wants to know a secret,

Dion and all my friends in the Ether

And of course to Emil, who cast a spell over me!

With love

Contents

Introduction

If you had the opportunity to read my first book, *5 Easy Steps to Becoming a Witch*, you will, hopefully, have learned the basics needed to start you on your witchy journey. Good for you – how great is that?! Now this is the next step to understanding more about your witchy self and where your talents lie, so that as you discover and empower yourself further you will automatically gain access to secrets that are specifically designed for YOU!

To use Sexy Spells, is to become a Sexy Sorceress and concentrate wholly on the wonder and magick of love. Becoming a Sexy Sorceress is all about tapping into your own special powers of enchantment and finding out what kind of a Witch you are and where your enchantments can lead you. So, for example, if at heart you are a Ditch Witch and you are wearing colours for a Ritch Witch, it is possible to get your wires crossed slightly (that is unless you want to be a Ritch Ditch Witch, which is a combination of the two!) Find the colours, magicks and areas special to you and then all your spellworking will have extra power within it. A Sexy Sorceress is a strong, confident person, male or female, who knows the secrets of their own particular power and uses them to make sparks fly and wonderful feelings inflame the most boring of days! Success to you, Sorceress – you have the Power!

As a working example of how you can acquire secret knowledge, there is a well-known word hidden within this book, which is a magickal word that can bring you success in your spellworking whenever you correctly call upon its power! However, the word is hidden and must be used in the right way and it is up to you to find it and work out how to use its power of enchantment. Nothing is ever explained completely in witchcraft because one of the essential ingredients of increasing your powers is the interest, research and originality that must be developed by you. **Every Witch's power is special to that Witch alone because the Wiccan way is all about developing YOU and your powers, rather than following set rules.** Of course, there is basic information that we must all research and learn about. However, ultimately, the way to make your magick work is to find your own power, using whatever knowledge you can acquire (whether it be from ancient sources, books or practice), and then *make* it work yourself rather than exactly copying others.

This word that I have mentioned is well known in magickal circles and can be found in the text of this book; it is hidden within other words and pictures and explanations and if you seek, you will find it. Once you have worked out the magickal power of this word and the possibility of great success is at your fingertips, then you too should keep this knowledge a secret! The only way for others to find it is to search and so **the secret of the magick is contained, but the answer is known** and you yourself have found it! To give you a hint and start you off, the word is best used in conjunction with the four secret names of the Elements. By harnessing their power in combination with the secret word and with the correct ritual (that you will find in this book) you can call success to your door. Use this knowledge wisely, it is a great gift for these times.

There's quite a difference between a basic Hedge Witch and a Sexy Sorceress and it's up to you whether you want to concentrate on being one, the other or even both! We all have a bit of the Sexy Sorceress within us, but it takes some doing to bring her out and to benefit from her particular skills! A basic Hedge Witch is generally an all-round mystic, healer and spellworker, whereas a Sexy Sorceress is more concerned with one particular area of life – and that is the power of love! Her exciting and sexy nature harks back to the time when cool Witches were wild (and free to be wild), and her skills are one of the most ancient skills of all. **Of course, men are just as able to be Sexy Sorceresses as women but for the purpose of explanation I have focused on the female, because once men have accessed their feminine power, they are on the same level, so can be called female too!**

If you feel that at heart you *are* a Sexy Sorceress, you have learnt one of the most important lessons of life already – and that is **love**. Love is the secret energy that all Witches know about and that all Sexy Sorceresses are concerned with, making them rulers of the world! Love is essential in this world and if you have the keys to love, you have the keys to power and magick itself! It's not easy developing and sustaining your skills (like all things to do with magick, it takes practice), but if you have the call, you will succeed! First of all you need to know which steps to take and in which direction to go. So that is what this book is about: Sexy Spells for a Sexy Sorceress! After that, it's up to you, Tiger!

So mote it be!

Gilly Sergual.

Chapter One

The Look!

It is not my intention to dictate to anyone how they should dress or look – the great thing about being a Witch is that each person is a law unto themself and originality is to be encouraged. However, appearance is important when you are 'tapping into' the Ether, because different colours, fabrics and shapes all have an effect on the energy around us. If we can find the Look that connects with our spiritual look, it hooks us up more readily into the other side by giving off our particular and individual cosmic 'signature'. Don't worry about your shape, size or natural inclinations – don't worry if you're outwardly male or female – the Look covers everyone and is divided into many different areas for different types. Below are described the four basic types, although taking a bit of each look is usually the best way for a Witch to find her own unique individuality. First, however, find your type.

Air

Magick name for Air: Esarp

(I'm a sensitive airy Niche Witch)

These Sorceresses traditionally look best in sheer, see-through chiffon and with bare feet or the very minimum of strappy shoes! As the fabric floats and moves around their bodies, so do their Air qualities. Their perfect designer would be Zandra Rhodes or Jasper Conran. Air Sorceresses tend towards a light-hearted and non-involved personality and this is because they are usually quite sensitive souls and can be hurt easily, so as a form of protection they skip about in relationships, attracting attention but doing their very best not to get tied down!

* **Best colours:** silver, white, pale blue, lilac and accents of grey
* **Special stones:** pearl, amethyst, moonstone and green topaz
* **Perfect perfume:** Envy by Gucci and Allure by Chanel
* **Ace aftershave:** Happy by Clinique and Men by Tommy Hilfiger

Ritch Witch

Fire

Magick name for Fire: Beetom

(I'm a vibrant fiery Ritch Witch)

These Sorceresses often look best in rich, warm, figure-hugging velvets with high-heeled court shoes or sexy boots! As the fabric clings and ignites their passion, this emulates their Fire qualities. Their perfect designer would be Versace or Vivienne Westwood. Fire Sorceresses are so hot they often burn up the relationship before it has had time to develop and this is because of their passionate belief in doing what they feel is right despite the many rules of courtship! They need to concentrate on simmering the love so that it doesn't burn out!

- **Best colours:** red, pink, orange, purple and accents of gold
- **Special stones:** ruby, garnet, bloodstone or jet
- **Perfect perfume:** No 5 by Chanel and Opium by Yves St Laurent
- **Ace aftershave:** Acqua di Gio by Giorgio Armani and Desire by Alfred Dunhill

Kitch Witch

 *Water*

Magick name for Water: Hacoma

(I'm an emotional watery Kitsch Witch)

These Sorceresses tend to look best in shiny satin and delicate lace with soft, embroidered or beaded, low-heeled slipper-type shoes. As the fabric ripples and drips over them, it enhances their Water qualities. Their perfect designer would be Dolce and Gabbana or Christian Dior. Water Sorceresses are usually incredibly emotional and tend to mix love and emotions into a whirlpool of uncertainty. This is because they get caught up in the flood of emotions and forget the moment! They should remember their best strategy is to keep cool!

- ❋ **Best colours:** turquoise, opal, navy blue, aquamarine and accents of copper
- ❋ **Special stones:** jade, emerald, sapphire and opal
- ❋ **Perfect perfume:** Image by Cerruti and Women by Paul Smith
- ❋ **Ace aftershave:** L'eau d'Issey Homme by Issey Miyake and Floris by Floris

Ditch Witch

Earth

Magick name for Earth: Nhanta

(I'm a natural earthy Ditch Witch)

These Sorceresses often look their best in leather and (faux) animal fur and wearing clumpy boots or shoes with laces that tie up their perfect legs! The sensual nature of leather and the hint of strength encourages their Earth qualities. Their perfect designer would be Fendi or Prada. Earth Sorceresses lean towards quick-witted and dominating personalities. They like to get involved deeply and carry on the relationship, refusing to give up until it is truly dead and buried. This is because of their intense belief in the power of love once they've decided on a mate! They should remember to let the relationship grow in its own natural way.

- ❊ **Best colours:** green, brown, yellow, black and accents of bronze
- ❊ **Special stones:** onyx, amber, agate and diamond
- ❊ **Perfect perfume:** Intuition by Estée Lauder and Truth by Calvin Klein
- ❊ **Ace aftershave:** Le Male by Jean Paul Gaultier and Eternity by Calvin Klein

Hair

Hair is a naturally occurring gift that most of us have and even if it has all fallen out, you can still buy a wig! Hair is very important because it is a magickal energy source by itself! (Remember what happened to Sampson when Delilah cut his hair? Or how Rapunzel used hers to escape from the tower? Remember how every Witch should have a hank of hair for spellworking? And so on ...) Let's suppose that you are lucky enough to still have your own hair, here's what to do with it!

A lot of Witches believe that keeping it long is best. For a Sorceress there is nothing easier to attract a mate than by swishing long, groomed hair ..t them! Long hair is sexy because it calls to the animal within us all and suggests that ancient wildness. You can drape a fringe over part of your face and subconsciously send out a message that there is something secret about you. You can tie your hair into complicated knots and expose the back of your neck – a very exciting area of the body that is often hidden and therefore revealing it can release a very secret and potent attraction power. Hair can be curled (wild and free), plaited or cut short (youth and domination), coloured (crazy and experimental) or simply

kept in the best, glossiest and
richest condition (pure sex!).
Work on your hair – get it
looking its best and you
have one secret weapon at
hand already!

If you don't have hair – don't despair!
There are some fantastic wigs around.
Or if you dislike wigs then how about
tying a glamorous headscarf in
gorgeous fabric around your head?
How about a tattoo on your head
– is that too radical? Then think
about the wonderful hats around.
If you're still not satisfied, then
make a choice – either go with
your beautiful naked head and be
proud of it or get spellworking
Witchy and grow your hair back!

Make-up

*E*ven for a natural Witch, there is nothing wrong with make-up! A lot of people tend to think if a Witch has make-up plastered all over her face ... (well, something derogatory!) That is not the case! Luckily, now that society is chilling out a little more, it is OK to be seen with wild and extravagant make-up, but to start with let's be a little more subtle. Remember the ancient saying: 'Slowly, slowly catch the monkey!' (and believe me, the only animal I'm alluding to here is the one inside your lover!)

The most important aspects of make-up are to enhance your own unique attractions. So if you have problem skin, for example, and want to hide it, then foundation of some sort is a must for you – whether it be simple concealer for under the eyes, or full-blown powder and paint! Lips are the next most important area because, as any Sexy Sorceress will tell you, that's where most of the attention is paid. Lipstick helps make them big and luscious and before you know it, you'll be having a queue of admirers desperate to kiss it off! Lipgloss is a great friend of the mouth! The wet look of a big shiny mouth is sure to get you noticed. Lipliner, however, should be handled with care as the 'dark edge filled in with light' is an absolute no-no! Keep the liner and lipstick either the same shade of colour or a close variation. Then, after drawing the line, you should ideally smudge in the lipstick, blot and finish with a good slick of gloss – and then some! Eyelashes next; you've got to have lots of these if you want to bat them at people! Mascara, eyeliner, false eyelashes and glitter – these are all essential for making your eyes a clear window to your soul! Eyes can hypnotize and spellbind so it stands to reason that you, as a Sexy Sorceress, should concentrate on them! Cheekbones, thinner noses and chins, and larger cleavages can all, believe it or not, be disguised with the correct make-up, so you see

how necessary it is! Important points to remember are always: dark colours make aspects diminish and recede and light colours make aspects larger and more prominent. Sparkles and glowing make-up draw attention, and matte make-up turns attention away! Smelling nice is of paramount importance to a Sexy Sorceress – it is an important calling card. Whenever your love smells that smell, they will think of you – so get it right!

There are beauty places and some brand-name chemists (or drugstores) that give free make-up lessons (and of course there are always books); so if you're not entirely sure about how to do it, get some advice first and then practise, practise, practise!

 Shoes

Shoes (or the lack of shoes) are a great weapon for attracting attention! Lovers can be fascinated by feet. Black, high-heeled stilettos are the obvious magnet that most lovers are drawn to (it's not necessarily a power thing but more likely a wish that they themselves were wearing them!). But any shoe with a strap around the ankle not only looks sexy but draws attention to the smallness of your ankle (even if it isn't that small!). Colour co-ordinating footwear with your clothes is a neat trick – it makes you look taller because the eye focuses on the colour and fills in the leg bit!

Low heels can be just as sexy as high – it's all about how you wear them. For example, if you're wearing a lacy, minidress with black tights and a thick pair of clod-hoppers this will give you a cutesy-girlie look, whereas if you wear sheer stockings and a pair of very elegant high heels, you will have a sex-goddess look! It's up to you. Remember, however, if you are going barefoot, a Sexy Sorceress will always, always, paint her toenails first!

P.S. If you're a man – believe me on this one – you never, *ever*, wear socks with sandals!

Accessories

In the days of my grandmother, the only accessories a Witch needed were a hat, bus fare or broomstick home and a clean hankie (and the latter was usually stuffed in a knicker leg)! Thank goodness times have changed. I can't imagine for a minute going out with just a hat and a hankie – and neither can any other self-respecting Sexy Sorceress! Accessories are tricks of the trade, useful tools and magickal accoutrements – so, in my mind, the more the merrier! If you have a small handbag, then your accessories should match accordingly, if you have a large handbag – then go for it big time! It's all a matter of balance. So, if you are wearing a particularly exotic outfit, then your jewellery and shoes for example, should be simple and plain. A lily needs no gilding. However, if you've gone for an LBS (little black suit) then you can go crazy with huge pearl neck chokers, silver wrist bands and tassels on your Manolos! The balance code is simple: one exotic outfit = lots of simple accessories or one simple outfit = lots of exotic accessories. Wear belts tight if you have a tiny waist, wear them loose if you have a large waist and don't wear them at all if you have no waist! Simple!

Although it is great if you can follow one type of elemental style, most of us are made up of varying degrees of all the Elements, so it is more probable that you will want to mix a few of the Elements together – and that is perfectly OK! Remember always that as you follow these Sexy Spells, you will become more and more in tune with who you are and who you want to be, so if your heart calls out strongly for a mixture of leather and lace –

YOU GO, GIRL!

Chapter Two

The Attitude!

So you have practised the Look and you're feeling good, now before you go out there you have to have the Attitude! This is all about **courage, confidence and communication**. With the three Cs hidden away in your bag, you are taking definitive steps into the world of the Sexy Sorceress.

Let's take **courage** first. In order to be a Sexy Sorceress, you need a bag full of courage! Unfortunately, it's not just about carrying a velvet bag with a courage spell in it! It has to come from within your soul and most of us find courage a bit of a handful. Courage takes practice – so start off slowly and then venture further as your courage grows. If your courage fails you at the last moment, realize that this is a natural event. Pat yourself on the back for coming so far and then retreat until you have the courage under control again. Courage is NOT about forcing an issue, it's about feeling right about an issue! Courage takes time to master and if it takes all your courage to talk to the 'sex-on-a-stick' at school or to go down to the local bar – then you are not quite ready for a date in that trendy night-club! Courage likes friends, so if you have a few friends to go about with, then all the better. But be warned: courage often goes off with friends and deserts you when you need it most – so make absolutely sure that what you are feeling, comes from deep within. That way, it is a lasting

courage and one that will protect and serve you best!

Confidence is first cousin to courage and walks with it hand in hand. It's all very well having the courage to talk to your love or go into your local bar, but if, once you've achieved that, you then dissolve into nervous giggles or drink too much, then you are not a behaving like a Sexy Sorceress! Grab confidence and give it a good shake, after all, you *are* a Sexy Sorceress! A regular positive message to yourself, delivered whilst looking in a mirror will do wonders for your confidence. Every morning, look into your mirror and tell yourself, *'I am gorgeous, I am clever, I am bright, there is nothing I cannot do if I want to, I am a Sexy Sorceress!'* If you do this enough, it will sink into your subconscious and, before you know it, your confidence will be flying high! A trick to remember, which works well when it looks as though your confidence might be waning, is to remind yourself when you walk into a room full of people: *they are not looking at me – they are all worrying about who could be looking at them!* Once you've changed the point of view from *your* worries to *their* worries, confidence returns and you can walk into that room full of compassion – everyone there is thinking about themselves and, after all, you are a Sexy Sorceress who doesn't worry a bit! People are always attracted to confidence – so it is well worth practising and getting right – if the worst comes to the worst and you suddenly panic as your confidence unexpectedly deserts you in the middle of a group conversation, then just make an excuse and dash to the bathroom! Highly effective – no loss of confidence in going to the bathroom and once you're there, there's usually a nice big mirror to practise your mantra in before returning to the party! *Et voilà!*

Communication is essential once you've mastered courage and confidence because you've got the courage to go to the party, the confidence to walk up to Mr Gorgeous and now ... er ... umm ... bother! ... can't think of what to say. Hmmm. The trick with communication is to listen first to what the other person is saying (or at least look as though you're extremely interested!) and then when you get a chance to speak – make sure you sound as if you know what you're talking about! It doesn't have to be a conversation about brain surgery or anything highly skilled – you can talk about the weather as an opening line (after all, it puts a lot of people at their ease if you march up and brightly say, 'What awful weather we're having!' with a big grin on your face! They immediately feel at ease dealing with a subject matter that everyone can talk about! Clever you!) If by any chance there is an uncomfortable pause – perhaps you marched up at the wrong moment when Mr Gorgeous was talking about his ex-wife's alimony (weather conversations wouldn't really go down well at that moment) – do not panic! Simply fill the awkward gap with something like, 'Sorry! I didn't mean to barge in, but it's absolutely peeing down out there and I've just slipped over!' with a big smile of course. This immediately breaks the tension with 'sorry', then causes amusement with 'peeing down', and leads to compassion and involvement with 'I've just slipped over'. Ha! Forget the alimony discussion, you, the Sexy Sorceress, have just swiftly turned everything to your advantage! (If, by any chance, after all that it still hasn't worked and you're being stared at like a particularly nasty piece of chewing gum – remember the bathroom trick and dash off for a pee and a grin in the mirror!)

Chapter Three

The Know How!

Once you feel you've got the hang of these three essentials, then you are ready to develop **your Know How skills**. A Sexy Sorceress, or Witch of any kind, has no time for negativity – this brief visit to the world has to be full of positive energy, laughter and good times. If your life currently seems full of negativity, it is you yourself who has the power, within you, to change it – and, once you decide to change your life, you can hear the Angels cheering you on from the uppermost reaches of the Ether. Believe me when I say that if things go well, the Spirits cheer and if things go bad, they weep with you and are close by, urging you not to give up but to keep trying. This unseen force will eventually strengthen your own determination, and as your powers and knowledge grow, so will your good fortune, love and laughter.

Widdershins

Widdershins is the Witches' term for the direction of anti-clockwise and follows the path of the Moon in the sky. Widdershins connects you to the Female Goddess aspect, the left-hand side, and is used for starting and beginning things, opening things and going back in time when spellworking.

Deosil

Deosil is the Witches' term for the direction of clockwise and follows the path of the Sun in the sky. Deosil connects you to the Male God aspect, the right-hand side and is used for finishing and ending things, closing things and going forward in time when spellworking.

Sigils

Sigils are symbolic drawings, illustrations and symbols that are found everywhere and in every time. They are symbols that affect the molecules around and within everything and, as such, create magickal flow. As you look deeper into the meanings and reasons behind sigils, the knowledge that you acquire empowers your understanding and working with sigils brings immediate and satisfying results.

 The Hey

The Hey is an ancient symbol that looks like two circles joined together or a figure of eight lying on its side. It can be portrayed in any manner: for example, written in ink, drawn in the air with a magick wand, cut into food, made out of stones, salt or flowers, cut into sand, laid out in candles, and so on. If there are enough of you, you can even make the symbol by standing and holding hands – as in all things, you must find the way that works best for you. The Hey symbol is a powerful sigil of communication between our two worlds of Matter and Spirit. It is very useful when contacting spirits or spellworking and I like to think of it as a doorway or speakerphone to the other side! (Don't be surprised though if Aports (materializations) drop through from time to time!)

You can construct a permanent Hey on or around your Altar or you can draw one up each time when working within your Magick Circle – it's entirely up to you. For a perfect Hey, draw it three times, from left to right, right to left and then upright. A lovely thing to do if you have a space of your own is to construct a permanent Hey. As a basic Hey image, I would suggest drawing a Pentacle first for protection and then in the middle draw the image of the Hey and decorate it with whatever bits and pieces you like. You can draw your Hey straight onto a wall or construct it first on a piece of wood or cardboard. You can build it on the floor or on the ceiling – it's entirely up to you. Once your Hey has been constructed and blessed in your own particular way, it will remain always a door to the other side.

The Magick Circle

This is a protective sphere, orb or circle conjured by your magick wand or athame (Witches' knife) if you prefer. Like the Hey it can also be made of natural objects, such as stones, flowers or salt, and can be delineated by candles – small tealight candles are best for this. I draw the circle widdershins but you can do deosil if it feels better for you. Draw the circle in three batches of three times with your magick wand in the air, envisioning a glowing light of blue, purple and white flowing from your wand, saying, 'By the power of three times three, I draw a magick circle around thee and me.' Wave the wand three times in whichever direction you prefer and repeat this each time. Stop for a moment and envision the bright light forming a protective sphere around you. Then repeat the exercise another three times and then another three times, all the time picturing the circle growing stronger and more impenetrable around you, until finally it becomes a huge circular globe that not only surrounds you but that reaches far up into the Ether and down into the Earth.

You are now in your magick circle of power. As you then do your spellworking and rituals, the magickal energy (prana or chi if you prefer) will become imbued with power and this is what you use to make your magick successful. Repeat the ritual in the opposite direction three times three times, when closing the circle, saying,

'By the power of three times three, I close this circle from around thee and me.' Finally, end by thumping the ground three times with your left hand, saying, 'Blessed be, Amen.'

 The Pentacle

Penta means five. The Penta-cle or Penta-gram is a five-sided figure of a star, or a star within a circle. It is a very ancient symbol and a very strong protective sigil. The Pentacle can be interpreted as a symbol of the Goddess within the Universe. It can also mean the Universe within the embrace of the Goddess. The circle is symbolic of the circular spirit of life; the star is symbolic of the star-like Matter of life. When the two symbols are joined into one sigil this makes a

powerful and potent force used for protection purposes and power. Witches make the sign of the Pentacle with their whole bodies and this is where the pointy hat and shoes come in handy! You stand with feet apart and arms raised wide above your head. The Witches' hat has a point that is one end of the star, long fingernails are the two other points on the end of each hand, and pointed shoes are the final two points on the end of each foot – making a total of five star points that connect you with the sacred symbol! Another way to make the sign of the Pentacle on your body is to draw it with your hands (*see page 166*).

Solomon's Seal/ Star of David

This is another star, but this time with six sides. It is composed of two triangles: one pointing upwards, which is representative of Male, God, Sun, Matter; and one pointing downwards, which is representative of Female, Goddess, Moon, Spirit. The two triangles are imposed one on top of the other to make the six-sided star. It is the unity of the two halves again, but this time concerned with the two opposites; male and female, as opposed to the (five) Elements. This star is a perfect combination of Yin and Yang and is used wherever duality or the power of two is needed in a spell.

 Numbers

Numbers are very important; they hold the keys to the Universe and are used in many ways to effect magick. You will find particular numbers that relate to you or strings of numbers that are relevant to your workings, but in essence the basic knowledge of the first 10 numbers is listed opposite. So now when you are practising your magick, incorporate the numbers that are relevant to what you are doing. For example, if you are spellworking to bring feminine power to a love potion, it would be best to use the number six in your rituals rather than seven, because seven is essentially a masculine number. Similarly, if you are doing a healing spell, for example, then incorporating the number two (balance) with four (magickal life force) would probably be the most effective combination. However, once again, it is up to you to research the meanings and powers behind the numbers and use them as YOU will.

0 The serpent swallowing her tail. The eternal circle of life – life, death and rebirth.

1 The One. The Primal Androgene – power of the Feminine Principal.

2 Goddess and God, Yin and Yang, light and dark, Matter and Antimatter, Spirit and Soul, balance.

3 The Triformus aspect of the Goddess – Maid, Mother and Crone. The Trinity – Goddess (life), Consort (death) and Son (rebirth of Consort).

4 The Elements – Earth, Air, Fire and Water. The Archangels – Michael, Gabriel, Auriel and Raphael. The Saints – Matthew, Mark, Luke and John. Balanced Totality of the Moons – Full Moon, Dark Moon, New Moon and Crescent showing how the Creation began; primeval waters, darkness, magickal force and hidden times.

5 Pentacle. The four Elements plus Spirit, embraced by the Goddess.

6 The sacred number of the Goddess – Maid, Mother and Crone plus the Trinity. Also the six spheres in the Earth's underworld.

7 The sacred number of the God. Seven main chakras. Good luck and fortune. Also the seven spheres in the Sky's upperworld.

8 Totality of Moons and magickal life force intensified. The Ogdoad – eight Gods and the eight spokes of the magickal life-sphere sigil.

9 Three times three – ultimate and extreme protection.

10 The One plus the Eternal Circle – extreme power.

 Words

*W*ords contain power – from the number of letters in a word, the way it is pronounced and the strength with which it is delivered, the feeling behind a word, its positive or negative essence, whether it is a female or male word and so on. Since ancient times people have believed that if you knew a thing or person's true name you had power over them. A few ancient and magickal words and names used in spellworking are shown as follows:

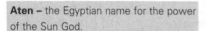

Aten – the Egyptian name for the power of the Sun God.

Goddess – to call upon the Goddess will always bring results.

Love – in the name of love and by the power of love all spells should be made.

Amen – to close spellworking, calling on the Egyptian God Amun.

Agla – an ancient word that calls success to your workings.

Hey – the symbol of the Hey bought to life by pronouncing its name.

Nhanta – the magick name of the Earth element.

Esarp – the magick name of the Air element.

Beetom – the magick name of the Fire element.

Hacoma – the magick name of the Water element.

Ho – a powerful word to call something into action and end a spell.

Toth – God of magick.

Astroarche (Libera) – Goddess and Queen of Stars.

Astraea (Maat) – Goddess and Queen of Justice.

Castor – Sun God rising.

Polydeuces – Sun God setting.

Hecate – Goddess of Witches and the crossroads of spirits and energy.

Ankh – life – male and female union.

Wicce – (feminine) wise woman.

Wicca – (masculine) wise man.

Wiccian – to bewitch.

Wiccan – Witches; practitioners of Witchcraft.

Hexen – ancient name for Witch.

Hex – spell.

Glamor – spell.

Blessed be – Witches' blessing.

As I will – so mote it be – Witches' statement making magick work through the power of the will.

And of course, the magickal word that I mentioned at the beginning of this book, which is hidden in the above list.

Air, Fire, Earth and Water

If you call upon the Elements for their help and support in your spellworking, they will empower your abilities with a great force. They are your siblings – your two great sisters and your two great brothers – and their power is seen in everything that shapes the cosmos. To explain further, they can be divided into equal columns encompassing many attributes. These attributes are what you look for individually when composing a spell and then use the correct Element or Elements to help you relate to your particular needs. Most things can be divided up into the four main Elements and below are a few ideas to start you thinking of what else corresponds likewise.

Air	Fire	Earth	Water
Crescent Moon	Full Moon	Dark Moon	New Moon
Priestess	Mother	Crone	Maid
Zeus	Hephaistos	Hades	Poseidon
blue	red	green	white
sapphire	ruby	emerald	diamond
incense	candle	cauldron	chalice
Raphael	Michael	Auriel	Gabriel
John	Matthew	Luke	Mark
Ostara/Beltane	Litha/Lamas	Mabon/Samhain	Yule/Imbolg
Spring	Summer	Autumn	Winter
Esarp	Beetom	Nhanta	Hacoma
breath	temperature	skin	sweat
masculine	masculine	feminine	feminine
magick wand	scourge	staff	athame
sky	mountains	caves	sea
scent	blood	food	liquid

The Goddess and the God

All Goddesses are the one Goddess. She has many names and many images but She is the One Feminine Principal from where all magick comes. Similarly, all Gods are one God. He too has many names and forms but he is always the Consort of the Goddess, and, during the cycle of life, he transmutes through death and rebirth into the Son. 'The Night of the Mother' – Modranect – was the pagan celebration of Yule held on the eve of 20 December and the following days, 21 December and 22 December. It was the night that the Mother Goddess gave birth to the God and so, from a Witch's point of view, the beginning of the Pagan year. However, traditionally Witches prefer the ancient pagan Samhain festival as the end of the old year and the beginning of the next. The Goddess is variously known as:

White	Red	Black
Maid	Mother	Crone
Isis	Hathor	Nephthys
Ana	Babd	Macha
New Moon	Full Moon	Dark Moon
15 years	30 years	60 years

She who is worshipped by the Witches as Hecate.

The Goddess, a three-fold, Sea, Earth and Moon deity (Maid, Mother and Crone) ruled with Her consort the (horned) God, attuned to the Sun. The God was born at Modranect as the Son, grew throughout the year and then transmuted into the Consort of the Goddess at Midsummer Solstice when he impregnated the Goddess with himself and then was sacrificed and died. The year carried on through the different Moon months until the Goddess gave birth at Modranect, again, to the Son. So the wheel-cycle of life would continue, through birth, death and re-birth. The reason so many ancient Pagan sites have a common marker for the Midsummer Solstice and the Midwinter Solstice is that these were the two most important events in the Pagan cyclical wheel of life. The Summer Solstice was when the God impregnated the Goddess and the Winter Solstice was when the God was reborn to the Goddess.

 Angels

Pagans and Witches the world over know that the original beliefs, times of celebrations and even the symbols themselves – the cross, the re-birth of God, his sacrificial death, and the Goddess as Mother – were all Pagan in origin. Take angels, for example; although they can take any shape or form and are divided into many different types, the main nine titles of the recognized hierarchy are thought to be: SERAPHIM (having six wings, two over the face, two over the feet and two used for flying – these are angels of pure love); CHERUBIM (usually thought of as cute and child-like types with wings – they are in fact fully grown human shaped with two wings on each side and are angels of pure knowledge); THRONES, DOMINIONS, POWERS , PRINCIPALITIES, VIRTUES (metaphysical spirits of order and justice, energy and numbers); ARCHANGELS (highest ranking messengers and angels of the Elements), and ANGELS (communication). Then within each of the nine individual hierarchies there are hundreds of different angel aspects that one can commune with.

Names of angels are very powerful, and calling upon them specifically is to be encouraged as all of us are part of that same spiritual family, whatever religion or denomination we feel we belong to. For example, if you want to spellwork for financial help, there is absolutely nothing wrong in calling upon the particular angels connected to numbers and numerology – who knows what they might tell you! It is said in magick that 'one knows everything who knows how to count because numbers are the keys of the cosmos and, by knowing, humans will know themselves and the One'. So if you're interested in numbers for whatever reason, the angels to commune with are: URIEL, ABRAXAS, RUBIEL, MITHRA and BARACHIEL. The four Archangels who stand at the four corners of the cosmos and guard the Elements are known as: MICHAEL, angel of Fire; AURIEL, angel of Earth; GABRIEL, angel of Water; and RAPHAEL, angel of Air. Pagans and White Witches have long communed with them on matters such as healing, spellworking and magick – remember, you only have to call.

Dance Movements

A very important part of ritual is dance and, especially if you are learning to become a Sexy Sorceress, your dance is vital to your spellworking. Dance attracts fairies, stirs the Ether and lends power to your spellworking. Believe me, no one can ignore a Sexy Sorceress when she's dancing! A lot of dances are based around circular movements, following the path of the Moon or the Sun. Linking with people or objects adds power, and fast or slow movements get different results. Drawing symbols in the air as you spin will call the magick to you. I always like to dance with bare feet as the feel of the Earth beneath my feet is actually a potent aid in magick and gives a strong connection with the Goddess. Different rhythms attract different powers, and as you move slowly or fast you should be able to connect with the different powers you are tuning into. The more you practise your dances, the stronger your connections should become and the more in-tune you will be! As far as music goes – well that is a whole other book by itself! Music is life force and using sound to 'power up' spellworking is essential in every Witch's rituals. Listen carefully for the sounds that call to you.

Chapter Four

Sexy Spells to Get You Going!

Sexy Spells are not only for lovers you know! Sometimes even the most contented or the most lonely of people need a little something to add spice into their lives. So this collection of Sexy Spells is for every Sexy Sorceress, whether happy with a partner or not! Whether you need to welcome someone into your love life, help someone out of your love life, improve your sex life or create a great love affair, this collection of spells will start you off in the right direction and hold (nearly all) the answers – after that, it's up to you! Here, the Sexy Sorceress is concerned with only one thing; Sexy Spells – this is her very special talent, and yours also! Just find the spell that is relevant to your situation, put on your sexiest outfit and then bring the magickal winds and potent powers together to make you Queen of the Sexy Spell and winner in the game of love.

A few points to remember before starting your witchy skills are:

1. **Most important – you cannot enslave anyone, so if you have enticed a lover and it's not meant to be, then the spell will be *very* temporary. As a Witch you should already know that it is wrong to hold someone under a spell against their will, even if you *can* do it!**

2. There are worldly tricks to help you along the way. A glimpse of cleavage, for instance, always works for women, because men – no matter how strong willed – will always be drawn to a hint of bosom! Even some of my dearest male gay friends have found their eyes inadvertently slipping to blouse level and then lingering in fascination! Be subtle with this one though, nobody wants an eyeful!

3. Smiling is always an excellent love puller! Whether it's a big breezy confident smile, a shy demure sexy smile or a friendly 'I'm just a pal' smile, the automatic response of anyone is to smile back – so you're half-way there already!

4. Altar Oil is a necessity when spellworking and invoking, along with other mystical

recipes, such as Magickal Ink, Power Ink, Protection Powder and Mystic Water. Although, as a developing and skilled Witch yourself, you may prefer to develop your own particular strains of these, I have explained the basic ingredients to give you an idea of where you're going!

✺5 All the ingredients are available in your local chemist (or drugstore), health food shop or grocery store! I have tested all the spells and creams, but as always, if you are allergic to anything mentioned below, do not use it! Nut oils can always be substituted for vegetable and olive oils – use your magickal know how! Lecithin are nourishing granules that feed your skin; lanolin is a pale yellow pure cream that is used as a base for your ingredients; and rosewater and witch hazel are pure waters made from the distilled flowers, which you can make yourself or buy at most chemists (or drugstores).

 Altar Oil

* 3 teaspoons of olive oil
* 3 teaspoons of rose oil
* 3 teaspoons of almond or walnut oil
* 1 acorn (male)
* 1 rosebud (female)
* 1 frankincense incense stick

In a glass bottle, drip 3 teaspoons of olive oil, 3 teaspoons of rose oil and 3 teaspoons of almond or walnut oil. Shake bottle and then add 1 acorn (if you are male) or 1 rosebud (if you are female) and the ash from a burned frankincense incense stick. Shake vigorously before use. This oil is mostly used for anointing your third-eye area, with various sigils, when working within your circle, although it can be added to spells as an extra potent ingredient.

Magickal Ink

- ★ juice of beetroot
- ★ red food colouring
- ★ 6 drops of your own saliva

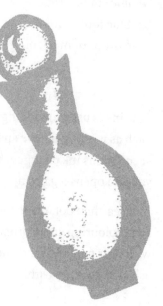

This ink is used for communication skills when spellworking; it is like writing directly to the Goddess or the Spirits in their particular ink. There are various different ingredients but the basic, start-you-off ink is the following.

In an earthen pot, drip: juice of beetroot, red food colouring and 6 drops of your own saliva. Stir with your athame and preferably use a willow stick to write with.

 Power Ink

- ★ juice of beetroot
- ★ blue food colouring
- ★ 6 drops of musk oil

This ink is used for adding power to spells, such as wishing or love spells. The colour and scent of this ink changes the molecules around you and opens a gateway.

In an earthen pot, drip: juice of beetroot, blue food colouring and 6 drops of musk oil. Stir with your magick wand and preferably use an ash stick to write with.

Protection Powder

★ 1 pinch of cumin seeds
★ 1 pinch of coriander seeds
★ 6 pips from a red apple
★ 1 pinch of silver glitter

This is very useful to have about, whether protecting your front door, telephone or computer or for doubling the protective strength within your magick circle.

Using a pestle and mortar, grind up equal halves of cumin and coriander seeds, 6 pips from a red apple and a pinch of silver glitter. Using your left hand, scatter wherever you need protection.

 Mystic Water

- ★ 2 fl oz (60 ml) witch hazel
- ★ 2 fl oz (60 ml) rosewater
- ★ 3 drops of lemon oil
- ★ 3 mint leaves
- ★ 1 handful of crushed basil
- ★ 1 handful of dried vervain leaves
- ★ 1 pint (600 ml) of water or 1 pint of pure vervain tea

In a glass pot, pour equal parts of witch hazel and rosewater. Add 3 drops of lemon oil, 3 mint leaves and a handful of crushed basil. Mix with dried vervain leaves and the water or pure vervain tea. Shake well and keep in a dark, cool place.

Mystic Water draws a very ancient power to you because of the ingredients and protects as well as enhances spellworking.

Finally, remember that you are a witchy Sexy Sorceress and as such, you have the automatic support of the Elements, the Goddess, Angels, and Spirits – so you *cannot* fail! Good hunting!

1. To make someone notice you

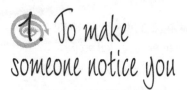

You know how frustrating it can be when you see someone you like and you're sure they (might) like you, but how to attract their attention? Well, the best and simplest way is to cast a gentle magick seal that should ensure their notice! Rose quartz is particularly good because it is attuned to relationships and emotions and smoky quartz is also good because it is attuned to the mind and drawing people to you.

You will need:

★ a pearl necklace (real ones are best but imitation will do)
★ 3 drops of musk oil
★ 1 pink rose
★ 1 small piece of rose quartz or smoky quartz
★ 1 stick frankincense incense

Best times:
Mondays, Friday and Sundays – Waxing or Full Moon

What to do:

Light the stick of frankincense and, in your cauldron, put the pink rose, 3 drops of musk oil and the piece of quartz. Using your athame (if you have one) turn the ingredients widdershins (anti-clockwise). Place pearl necklace in cauldron and say:

> *Power of the Lady*
> *Pearls of the South Sea*
> *I call upon this magick seal*
> *To make (name) notice me.*

Then take out the pearls and wear them around your neck. Take out the quartz and pass it through the incense smoke, saying:

> *Power of the Son and Lord*
> *Scent of magickal property*
> *Carry this seal within the Ether*
> *And make (name) notice me.*

Wash the cauldron in fast-flowing water and dry. Take the quartz with you (wearing the pearls) when going out. If you see someone you particularly like, try and give them the quartz or drop it in their pocket (do be careful not to look as if you're picking their pocket though!!)

2. To make someone contact you

For this spell, you should ideally have a crystal ball. However, finding your crystal ball can take some time and so, because the main gist of the spell is scrying, you can actually use any scrying medium, such as a pool of water, a mirror or even a highly polished stone. The good thing about the crystal ball is its quartz make-up, which results in very quick responses; however, if you know the basics of scrying and concentrate hard, you should be able to do this with any polished surface. If you're using a bowl of water, try and make sure the bowl is a dark colour, which should help your concentration. The art to scrying is to relax your eyes and let the pictures and images come. Try not to focus on any one thing until you have the whole image around you as you will probably find initially that the more you concentrate on one image, the more it floats away! Slightly crossing the eyes is said to be a useful tool to getting there, but the major influence is to relax and, once you're on the scrying level, it will be easy!

You will need:

- ★ crystal ball or scrying medium
- ★ gauze veil or piece of transparent material – preferably with hints of opaline colours woven into it
- ★ 3 basil leaves
- ★ Magick Ink
- ★ 1 black candle
- ★ 1 stick of frankincense incense

Best time:

Any time, but Dark Moon is best

What to do:

Make sure the candle is burning in a safe place, such as the hearth, so that it cannot fall over and set light to anything! Light the incense and take the 3 basil leaves. On the first leaf, inscribe with your athame, 'AGLA'; on the second leaf, inscribe with Magick Ink, 'ZACHARIEL'; and on the third leaf, inscribe with your saliva the Hey symbol.

Now burn the first leaf in the candle flame, saying:

● *Agla, Agla, Agla,*
I call to thee,
Open the doors of the spirit world
And call to (name) for me.

Burn the second leaf in the candle flame, saying:

● *Zachariel, Zachariel, Zachariel,*
I call to thee,
Open the doors of the spirit world
And ask (name) to contact me.

Burn the third leaf in the candle flame, saying:

● *Hey, Hey, Hey,*
I call to thee,
Open the doors of the spirit world
And show (name)'s face to me.

Place the veil over your face and head and look through the gauze deep into your crystal ball or scrying medium. Think about the one you want to contact and talk to them or write down whatever you see. The spell has now been set in motion and that person should now respond to your ethereal call. When you are finished, the candle stub, incense and any water used must be returned to earth.

3. To find a new love

You will need:

★ 1 quince fruit

Best time:

Any time

What to do:

Place the quince under your pillow
and before going to sleep gently
tap your head on the pillow six
times, saying:

Venus fruit bring this night to me
A new love's face that I may see
My lover, gentle, kind and true
In dreams of love direct from you.

Think of the fruit, sacred to Venus, Goddess of Love, as you
fall asleep. You have now set the wheels of love in motion.

4. To entice an old love

You will need:

* 1 quince fruit
* a piece of paper with the name of your loved one written upon it
* 1 white handkerchief

Best time:
Under a New Moon

What to do:
Take the quince and cut it in half, lengthways. Insert the paper with your lover's name on it between the two halves and then wrap it tightly in the handkerchief. Go out under the Full Moon and toss the parcel as hard as you can over your left shoulder. Do not look where it has fallen or try to find it – leave it to do its magick.

5. To keep a lover thinking of you (visualization)

You will need:

★ ylang ylang or jasmine incense

Best times:
Within your magick circle

What to do:
Sit in the middle of your circle, burning the incense and close your eyes. Imagine yourself walking backwards down seven steps and when you get to the bottom, keep walking backwards until you find yourself in a garden. Now picture your lover standing in the garden opposite you, smiling. Slowly walk towards him and notice a shimmering golden rope tied around his waist. Take the other end of the rope and tie it around your waist. If you move away or around the garden, the rope moves with you; it cannot break.

Now you know that, wherever you both go, you will be attached by the ethereal rope. Only you can sever the connection. Now choose to return to your circle, walking out of the garden and back up the seven steps – the rope simply expands and you are both joined until you decide to let go.

6. To end a lover thinking of you (visualization)

You will need:

★ peppermint incense

Best time:
Within your magick circle

What to do:

Light the incense and imagine the same scenario as the previous spell, where you enter the garden and see your lover attached by the golden rope, waiting for you. Look down and pick up a small perfect white sword that is lying on a rose. Now carefully cut the golden rope that is connecting you both with the white sword

and then place the sword point down in the ground next to the rose. Say goodbye to your lover and climb the seven steps back to the magick circle leaving your lover behind you

7. To keep your lover wanting more

You will need:

★ a photo of yourself and a separate
  photo of your lover
★ 3 red ribbons
★ runny honey

Best times:
New Moon to Full Moon

What to do:
Take the two photos and bind them
tightly, faces together, with the red
ribbons. Cover the package with runny
honey and bury it, preferably under an
apple or quince tree.

8. To keep your lover coming back

You will need:

- ★ an item of your lover's clothing
- ★ an item of your clothing
- ★ dried jasmine flowers
- ★ dried rose flowers
- ★ black tissue paper
- ★ 2 black ribbons
- ★ 1 black candle

Best time:

Any time

What to do:

Hide an item of his clothing, sprinkled with dried jasmine flowers and wrapped in some black tissue tied with one ribbon, under your bed or the side of the bed you sleep on. Hide an item of your clothing, sprinkled with dried rose flowers and wrapped in some black tissue tied with the other ribbon, under his bed or the side of the bed he sleeps on.

Now light the candle within your magick circle and say:

> Venus keep these souls intact
> Keep my lover coming back.
> Blessed be. So mote it be, Amen.

Snuff out the candle but keep it in your circle and whenever you feel your lover straying, relight the candle and repeat the ritual until the candle has totally burned down.

9. Attraction potion

This spell should only be done by people old enough to legally consume alcohol, because of the wine element and also because it effects a very powerful result! So be absolutely sure before you begin that this is what you want. In time, most spells wane, but this particular one has a very potent result so handle with care!

You will need:

★ 1 bottle of Bach Flower Remedies: vervain
★ 1 glass of extremely good wine, such as (white) Chablis or (red) Chateau Neuf
★ 1 chopped strawberry
★ 1 apple pip
★ 1 sugar lump

Best time:
First quarter to Full Moon, in a social setting, such as a party, bar or restaurant

What to do:

Mix the glass of wine with 9 drops of vervain in your cauldron. Add the chopped strawberry, apple pip and sugar lump. Using your athame, stir the mixture widdershins (anti-clockwise in the direction of the Moon) and whisper:

Vervain, magickal root of light,
Attract to me the one I sight.
With apple's love and sweet desire
Bring (name) to me with Venus' fire.
Vervain, magickal root of light,
Bring the one I love to me
tonight.

Strain the liquid into a small glass bottle and take it with you to the party or bar where your loved one is. Now you must share the potion together, exactly half each. Be absolutely sure you are with the one you want because once the potion has been drunk, the magickal forces are in play and if you look at anyone else whilst drinking it – you may attract more than one reaction!

10. Stardust hair shine

There are many excellent non-magickal remedies that have been recommended over the years for shiny hair, which range from taking Brewer's Yeast daily, to using a tin of lentil soup as a conditioner and even sprinkling corn flour in dry hair and thoroughly brushing it out!
However, here is one lovely Stardust Hair Shine that I thoroughly recommend!

You will need:

★ 4 tablespoons dried marigold flowers
★ 1 tablespoon apple vinegar
★ 9 tablespoons boiling water

Best time:
Any time

What to do:

Place the flowers, vinegar and boiling water in your cauldron and leave to soak for half an hour. Then strain into a glass bowl and take outside under the stars. Stand with your bowl raised to the night sky and say:

By the power of glittering night,
Enchant this potion with
beauteous light.
Stardust in form and shape so fine,
Cover my hair with magickal shine.

Now wash (and condition) your hair as normal, towel dry your hair and then rinse it thoroughly with the Stardust potion. Leave the liquid in your hair and dry as normal.

11. Magickal face mask for a special date

So you've got a special date. You're gorgeous (of course), but a little magickal help would not go amiss. So I suggest this fantastic face mask, which will not only illuminate your features but will add a special magickal glow that mesmerizes members of the opposite sex and if nothing else, will almost certainly get people commenting on how healthy you look!

You will need:

* ⭐ 1 egg
* ⭐ ½ teaspoon runny honey
* ⭐ 1 teaspoon lecithin (available from chemists [drugstores] or health food shops)
* ⭐ 1 teaspoon almond oil
* ⭐ ½ teaspoon of dried thyme leaves
* ⭐ 6 apple pips
* ⭐ equal parts of witch hazel and rosewater mixed together

Best time: Fridays and either on a Full or New Moon if possible

What to do:

Place the egg, honey, lecithin and almond oil in your cauldron. Mix them together with your magick wand (or a wooden spoon will do). Slowly add in the dried thyme leaves and mix to a paste. Take the apple pips and add each one to a paste, saying after each one:

 One apple for desire.'

'One apple love's fire.'

'One apple to excite.'

'One apple love's bite.'

'One apple for wonderment.'

'One apple love's scent!'

Now smear the cream over your face (be careful not to get it in the eyes!) and leave for 30 minutes. Wash off with a mixture of rosewater and witch hazel, and have fun!

12. To get what you want

The title of this spell sounds a bit precocious but, as a Sexy Sorceress you will already know, everything is transitory – ever changing. Even if you desire something virtually impossible, it's worth a try with this spell as probably once you've got it, you'll find that you don't really want it after all and it will flow off into the Ether! Remember, as long as it's a good desire, it's OK to get what you want!

Note: Although it is perfectly all right to cross-gender, it has been found that sticking to your own gender will render this spell more potent, so I have explained the two methods for male Sorcerers and female Sorceresses.

You will need:

* ★ a place where an oak tree grows (for men)
* ★ a place where an apple tree grows (for women)
* ★ 1 gold candle (for men)
* ★ 1 silver candle (for women)
* ★ red ink
* ★ white paper
* ★ black sealing wax
* ★ a small but exquisite offering, such as a perfect truffle chocolate, a gold/silver charm, a rosebud or tobacco

Best time:

The Dark Moon (one day and night before the New Moon)

What to do:

At 6 p.m. on the night of the Dark Moon, go to your tree and light your candle at the base. Then take the white paper, red ink and black wax. First, write a description of what you want in the red ink on the white paper and surround it with a heart shape. Second, seal the message with the black wax and imprint your right (men) and left (women) index finger print in the wax. Take the message and pass it slowly through the flame of the candle three times, saying:

*This is what I want
Please bring it to me
By the power of the Dark Moon
So mote it be.*

Then take your offering and pass it slowly
through the flame of the candle three
times, saying:

* *This gift that I bring*
  Please receive it from me.
  By the power of the Dark Moon
  So mote it be.

Next, bury your message and the
offering at the foot of the tree. Wait
for the candle to completely burn out,
sitting in the magickal glow of the Dark
Moon and concentrating on what you want.
When the candle has burned down
completely, thump the base of the tree
gently three times with your right hand
(men) or your left hand (women) and say
loudly, 'AMEN.'

13. To beautify yourself

There are times when no matter how lovely we are, we all need an extra boost to beautify ourselves and this is the ideal spell for that moment. Some of the ingredients may look difficult to find, but believe me, you'll find them. Start at your local chemist (or drugstore), try the health food shop or even your local supermarket. It is worth getting the ingredients because this is a cream that works wonders and once you've made it, you'll wonder how you ever did without it!

You will need:

★ ½ mashed avocado pear
★ 5 mashed strawberries
★ 1 tablespoon sesame seed oil
★ 2 tablespoons lanolin cream
★ 1 teaspoon lecithin granules
★ 4 tablespoons warm water
★ rosewater to wash off

Best times: Fridays or Wednesdays, during a Waxing to Full Moon

What to do:

Melt the oil, lanolin and lecithin in your cauldron, stirring all the time and then slowly add the warm water and continue stirring, saying seven times:

Beautify and blessed be.

Then add the crushed strawberries and avocado and liquidize or use an electric whisk until the mixture cools into a thick pale green cream, saying seven times:

Attraction cream to work for me.

Keep it in a glass jar somewhere dark and cool (like the refrigerator) and use sparingly as a face cream and body moisturizer. Leave it on for half an hour at a time and use witch hazel or the bath (!) to wash off the cream – the more you use it, the more fabulous you will be! As the cream cools, it becomes quite hard and waxy so you will only need a small amount at a time. It gives a powerful rose complexion to the face and you can feel the magick working! Be warned though, it should only last for one week, after that you must return it to the earth.

14. Irresistibility for special occasions

This works equally well for men as well as women but there are a few differences.

For men to attract women: make the symbol, pyramid point downwards.
For men to attract men: make the symbol, pyramid point upwards.
For women to attract men: make the symbol, pyramid point upwards.
For women to attract women: make the symbol, pyramid point downwards.

You will need:

★ I very red apple
★ I tablespoon runny honey
★ I tablespoon ground almonds
★ 3 drops of your own saliva

Best time:
Any day, but preferably during a Waxing to Full Moon

What to do:

Mix the honey and almonds together in your cauldron then place 3 drops of your own saliva into the mixture, and stir widdershins (anti-clockwise) six times with your left middle finger, saying:

🍂 *Scents of the Goddess I mix with me*
   And bring to this night
   irresistibility.

Take the apple and cut it with your athame (if you have one) horizontally – so that it shows the five-pointed star in the middle. Smear both halves with the honey mixture and taking the top half, draw the pyramid sigil on your body, making sure some

of the honey mixture adheres to the skin.

The female pyramid sigil is point downwards: draw honey over chest area and down to navel.

The male pyramid sigil is point upwards: draw honey over both thighs and up to the navel.

Take the lower half of the apple and join it to the upper half and then bury the whole apple in your garden, window box or a pot of earth and leave to do its magick! Now go out there and see how well your irresistibility works!

15. To make a wish come true

Whatever your wish may be – financial, love, power, success – a Sexy Sorceress does not wait for fate! If she wants something to come true, she just magicks it so! This spell takes some time to prepare, but using the correct times of the Moon will empower it best. If you wish to do this at any other time, that is OK too – remember to do what you feel is the most relevant for your workings. With this powerful talisman, you can practise on your own wishes and success be yours!

You will need:
- ★ a chicken's wishbone
- ★ gold leaf or gold coloured paint
- ★ clear varnish
- ★ 1 red ribbon

Best times:
Waning to Dark and Waxing
to Full Moon

What to do:

Wash the bone thoroughly in running water (preferably in a stream outside) but the tap will do. Dry on a windowsill for 3 days and nights during a Waning Moon to rid it of any negativity.

Cover the bone in gold leaf or paint and varnish. Leave on the windowsill for 3 days and nights during a Waxing Moon to empower positivity.

On the Full Moon, take the bone outside and tie a red ribbon to one of the legs of the bone and put it around your neck, saying:

Dearest mother of the Full Moon,
Grant me tonight a magickal boon.
With this talisman all problem ceases
And in riches and health my life increases.
Dearest mother, all glory to thee,
Empower my talisman and so mote it be!

Now place the bone in your wallet or purse and let the fun begin! If the bone breaks at any time, this means the magickal energy has been used up (did you wish for something huge?!), so then you should make another.

16: Good fortune talisman

You will need:

- ★ a piece of aquamarine
- ★ 1 small square of blue velvet material
- ★ 1 gold ribbon
- ★ 7 drops of frankincense oil
- ★ 1 frankincense incense stick
- ★ a snippet of your hair
- ★ 1 dried mint leaf

Best times:

Any day, but particularly on a Dark Moon (one day before the New Moon) or, if you can work out when it occurs by yourself; particularly good is at the time of the *Blue Moon*, which only happens four times per year and is a very ancient magickal time!

What to do:

Light the incense stick. Place the aquamarine in your cauldron add the 7 drops of frankincense oil, saying after each drop:

- Oil of Fortune draw to me.'
  'Oil of Wonder that will be.'
  'Oil of Secrets tell to me.'
  'Oil of Ether mote it be.'
  'Oil of Good things hear to me.'
  'Oil of Success make it be.'
  'Oil of Magick come to me.

Now throw in the snippet of your hair and the dried mint leaf. Take the burning incense stick and stir cauldron widdershins, saying:

- With aquamarine and mint
     and hair
  Draw to me Fortune from everywhere.

Leave the incense to burn out and when the contents are quite cold, gather them up and place them in the blue velvet and secure with the gold ribbon. Carry this about your person or in your bag.

17: Attraction magnet

The following magnets are all based around the same spell, but using different elements and ingredients, depending on their use. This is an excellent way to begin learning about the drawing powers of these magnets and you can go on with research to make your own magnets. Other magnets are made in other ways but for these purposes, the following magnets all follow a central theme.

You will need:

★ 1 orange candle
★ a piece of agate
★ rose oil

Best time: **Wednesdays**

What to do:

Inscribe your name down one side of the
candle and the person or item you wish to
attract down the other side, using a pin
or your athame. Place 7 drops of
rose oil in the top of the candle
and light. When the candle
starts to burn the inscription,
carefully drop liquid wax
from the candle onto the
piece of agate. Now leave
the candle to continue
burning until it either goes
out or burns completely
down. If any of the candle is
left, place it with your piece of
agate in your purse or wallet.

18. Love magnet

You will need:

★ 1 pink candle
★ a piece of copper
★ patchouli oil

Best time: Fridays

What to do:

Inscribe your name down one
side of the candle and your
lover's name down the other side,
using a pin or your athame. Place 7 drops
of patchouli oil in the top of the candle and light. When the candle
starts to burn the inscription, carefully drop liquid wax from the
candle onto the piece of copper. Now leave the candle to continue
burning until it either goes out or burns completely down. If any of
the candle is left, place it with your piece of copper about your
person.

19. Success magnet

You will need:

★ 1 blue candle
★ a piece of amethyst
★ frankincense oil

Best time: Thursday

What to do:

Inscribe your name down one side of the candle and a word to describe the success that you need down the other side, using a pin or your athame. Place 7 drops of frankincense oil in the top of the candle and light. When the candle starts to burn the inscription, carefully drop liquid wax from the candle onto the piece of amethyst. Now leave the candle to continue burning until it either goes out or burns completely down. If any of the candle is left, place it with your amethyst and carry it about your person.

20. Money magnet

You will need:

- ★ 1 gold coloured candle
- ★ a piece of amber
- ★ clove oil

Best time:
Sunday

What to do:

Inscribe your name down one side of the candle and the word 'AGLA' down the other side using a pin or your athame. Place 7 drops of clove oil in the top of the candle and light. When the candle starts to burn the inscription, carefully drop liquid wax from the candle onto the piece of amber. Now leave the candle to continue burning until it either goes out or burns completely down. If any of the candle is left, place it with your amber and carry it about your person.

21. De-spell attraction

Best time:
Tuesdays (for banishing and authority elements)

Although it can be lovely to be admired there are times when even the most compassionate of us can get fed up with the attentions of an unwanted admirer. In these cases, one of the spells you can do is the following, which should cool any lovesick ardour!

You will need:

★ peppermint oil
★ 1 red ribbon
★ something belonging to your unwanted admirer (such as a letter received, hair or nail clippings, a photo or a piece of clothing)
★ a pair of scissors

What to do:

Attach one end of the ribbon to the item relating to your unwanted admirer and the other end to your middle finger on the left hand. Take the scissors (or get someone to do this for you) and cut the ribbon in the centre, between your finger and the item. While you cut the ribbon, shout as loudly as you can:

(NAME) BE GONE FROM MY CIRCLE!

Now take the peppermint oil and put 3 drops over each end of the cut ribbon. Bundle up your admirer's end of ribbon and burn it in a safe fire. Bundle up your end of the ribbon and throw it into moving water, like a stream or river.

22. De-spell jealousy

You will need:

- ★ a green peridot gem
- ★ geranium oil
- ★ a pot of geranium flowers
- ★ 1 red candle
- ★ a piece of paper and a pen

Best times:
Tuesday or Saturday
(particularly good for
removing obstacles)

What to do:

Inscribe the name 'Michael' down one side of the candle and 'Saturn' down the other side with a pin or your athame. Place candle in a south-facing direction and write the name of the person who is causing the jealousy on the paper. Place it at the foot of the candle with the peridot on top of the paper. Place 3 drops of geranium oil on top of the candle and 3 drops of the geranium oil on the peridot. Light the candle and leave to burn down. When done, collect all the items left and bury in the pot of geraniums. You can safely leave this in your home or garden as the jealousy element has now been constrained and will have no power.

23. De-spell anger

Shell is well known for its calming quality and healing over moods and emotions. Its connection with the Sea Goddess is a vital part of this spell.

You will need:

* ★ 1 shell
* ★ 1 glass of water
* ★ 1 pinch of salt
* ★ a tray of sand

Best time:
Whenever anger is bothering you

What to do:

Sit in front of the tray of sand and taking the shell, use it to comb the sand from top to bottom and left to right six times. Whisper quietly at the same time:

> *Mother, Hecate, Goddess of the Sea, Direct this anger away from me.*

Now take the glass of water and drink one tiny sip and pour the rest over the sand, saying:

> *Water, purified, as from the Sea, Banish this anger away from me.*

Now throw the pinch of salt over the wet sand and then place the shell in the middle of the sand and imagine all the anger being directed to the shell and contained there. When you are ready and feel cleansed, take the whole tray and drop it into a pond or stream or the Sea itself, if you can – in any event, some kind of naturally occurring water. (In this particular case the sink isn't really strong enough to take this spell!)

24. De-spell bad luck or negative energy

You will need:

★ 1 whole clove of garlic
★ a pot of earth (at home) or a small clear bag of earth (if you are outside)
★ a piece of tourmaline or jet

Best times:
Thursday is best, but obviously whenever you are expecting to be around negative energy and need to de-spell bad luck, perhaps in a meeting

What to do:

Place the clove of garlic on top of the earth and set the pot on a windowsill (if at home) or place the bag in your right pocket (if going out). Keep a piece of tourmaline or jet in your left pocket at all times.

If you are experiencing a run of bad luck, keep the clove for one day and one night only. The garlic will have drawn the negative energy to it and the earth will ground it in one place.

If you are at a meeting, carry on as normal but when it is over bury the clove of garlic and earth in your garden or the waste bin. You must get rid of the enchanted garlic or you will be keeping a small, condensed packet of negativity in your pocket! The black tourmaline and jet are ancient cures to get rid of fear and protect against negativity so you can continue to carry those about you.

25. To pep up your sex life

You will need:

★ ylang ylang incense or jasmine incense
★ a glass of roses, yarrow flowers and ash leaves
★ pink candles
★ a small bottle of champagne
★ strawberries, chocolate and honey
★ a sprig of holly and a sprig of ivy, tied together with a piece of red satin and hidden under your bed

Best time: Whenever your sex life needs a boost!

What to do:

You may find some of these ingredients hard to find at first but it is worth persevering by going to a good garden centre or similar as the 'ethereal signatures' of these ingredients give off extremely powerful sexual magnetism! The combination of smells, foods, and magicks will be sure to aid you in your desire!

NOW, SEXY, USE YOUR
IMAGINATION!!!

26. Connecting to your lover's thoughts

You will need:

★ a pendulum with a clear crystal on the end

★ a piece of clear quartz crystal or your crystal ball

★ white paper with your lover's name on it

Best time: Any time

What to do:

Place the paper under your crystal ball or piece of crystal in the east-facing direction of your home. Hold the pendulum above it and allow it to swing freely. Intone:

Raphael, Angel, Guardian of Air,
I call to you to aid my prayer.
Bring to me my lovers thoughts clear,
Speaking in words of power near.
Raphael, Angel, Guardian of Air,
Love send to you for aiding my prayer.

Now close your eyes and meditate, imagining a picture of your lover standing in front of you talking. Try not to strain the imagery and let the words come no matter how strange they may sound. When the image finally fades away, thump the floor three times to ground the spell.

27. Love potion

This love potion is also known as a Gem
Elixir. Gem Elixirs can be made for any
purpose, the trick is to know which
gems attract or repel and their various
magickal properties. The liquids used
are also relevant to each gem, so you
need to do some homework first
before making them! However, to start
you off, here is a basic love potion that
is pure of heart and certain to enhance
your Sexy Sorceress image!

You will need:

★ 6 tablespoons of spring water

★ a rose quartz crystal

★ 3 pink rose petals

★ 1 paper coffee filter

Best time: Any time you want to enhance your powers of attraction

What to do:

Put the 6 tablespoons of spring
water in your cauldron, one by
one, saying after each one:

● *Love divine!'*
　'Love wine!'
　'Love supine!'
　'Love fine!'
　'Love bine!'
　'Love will be mine! ●

Now add the 3 pink rose petals
and the piece of rose quartz. Taking your magick wand, make the
symbol of the Goddess over the cauldron (a circle with a half-moon at
the top), and say:

● *Blessed be, bring love to me.* ●

Stay for a while in front of your cauldron, thinking of the love that you
want. When ready, pour the liquid through the filter paper into a
glass container and drink. Now go out there and be irresistible!

28. Strengthen your aura ritual

You will need:

★ 1 white candle
★ myrrh incense

Best time:
Whenever you need to
replenish your prana energy,
but during the Waxing Moon
is best

What to do:
Face north within your magick
circle. Using the middle finger of
your left hand, touch the third eye area
and say:

🍂 *Spirit of the Moon.* 🍃

Touch your stomach area and say:

🍂 *Spirit of the Earth.* 🍃

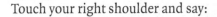

Touch your right shoulder and say:

🍃 *Spirit of the Sea.*

Touch your left shoulder and say:

🍃 *Spirit of the Sun.*

Bring your hands together in prayer form and point them high above your head and say:

🍃 *Mother Goddess, All of All of All,*
 May the power of your love be with me forever
 And increase my aura with strength and might.
 So mote it be, blessed be, Amen.

(Visualize your aura glowing with a strong gold and silver pulse as it attracts prana energy to it.) Lower your hands.

29. To ride a broomstick (elementary stage)

Riding a broomstick goes back in time a long, long way and crosses all continents, races and beliefs – it is the essential knowledge that every Witch should have. As can be expected, there has been a lot of nonsense and negativity attached to this ritual thanks to the 'dark ages'. But now that we are enlightened as a people I believe it is necessary to spread the word about this most mystical and enchanting ritual. There are many stages to riding the broomstick, but for the purposes of initiation, here is the elementary stage much used by me and my friends.

You will need:

- ★ a broomstick
- ★ a circlet of rosemary for your head
- ★ green tea with lemon
- ★ peppermint foot ointment
- ★ 1 black candle
- ★ frankincense incense

Best time: Whenever you fancy a lift!

What to do:

With naked feet and hair unbound, wearing your circlet made of rosemary on your head, cast your magick circle and place the broomstick on the floor pointing in the direction you wish to travel.

Light the frankincense incense and black candle. Cover your feet in peppermint foot ointment. Take a few sips of green tea with lemon and sit or lie on your broomstick, however you are comfortable, holding onto the pole. Close your eyes and breath steadily, concentrating on your breathing.

Now imagine that your body is floating upwards with the broom, but at the same time, your body is pushing downwards. (This sounds difficult, but once you get into the rhythm you should find it easy as pie!) You are achieving an undulating force within yourself. When you are happily moving both upwards and downwards at the same time in your mind, take a big leap in your thoughts and push yourself off the ground on your broom. Do not concentrate on what you are doing, just try and feel the freedom that this action brings and enjoy it!

You should now visualize the place you want to go in your mind's eye and as you fly, be semi-aware of the wind in your hair, the air rushing past you as you soar and the clean, cool feeling of being part of the spirit world. Whatever lovely positive thoughts spill through your mind as you fly, enjoy and laugh at them. (This helps to raise your feelings of power and confidence and continues your flight). If at any time you feel disconnected from what you are doing, try to visualize a gentle landing back to Earth and open your eyes, thump the ground three times and make the sign of the Pentacle. You can then start again! The more you practise this, the more your own abilities will come to the fore and the places you get to will simply rock your world! Happy flying!

30. To find your secret Witch's name – ritual

Finding your secret Witch's name is one of the most empowering moments in a Witch's life, because you officially become the child of the Goddess by receiving your name from Her. This name is then used with powerful effect when spellworking. We know that all names are important, but the secret name is given to you by the Goddess Herself and is your cosmic and universal signature that all the spirits will recognize. The name is given when you are ready to receive it, but if you are trying this ritual, you are obviously already at that stage! Don't worry if the result is not immediate – sometimes you can try too hard and then it comes when you finally relax(!) or other times you may not receive the answer in a dream as thought, but in some other place like a bookshop! The point is, when you are told your secret Witch's name, you will know immediately what it is. Finally, as you are probably already well aware; do not divulge this name to anyone – it is your special and secret link with the Goddess.

You will need:

★ frankincense incense
★ 1 white candle
★ 1 red candle
★ 1 black candle
★ a piece of white fabric with 'AGLA' written on it
★ a piece of quartz crystal

Best time:

When you are ready!

What to do:

Take a bath and purify yourself in your own way. Draw up your magick circle and light the three candles and frankincense incense. Tie the 'AGLA' fabric around your right hand and hold the crystal in your left hand. Sit or lie on the floor head pointing east.

Visualize standing by the edge of the Sea. Hear pounding waves and the noise of the sand crunching under your feet. In your mind, rise up, stretch yourself and will yourself to fly into the clouds. Notice how light you feel and the cool breeze around you. Now gently lower yourself to the ground and come to a stop upright, next to a beautiful bonfire. Look at the golden and red sparks that fly around and the embers of the wood glowing brightly in the flames.

In your mind, draw the Pentacle sigil around you and feel yourself turning into a flower returning to Mother Earth. Your feet become the roots and dig their way deep into the cool earth, your hands become leaves and your face is the face of a sunflower. Feel the breeze blowing your leaves, the light rain feeding you and the Earth nourishing you, the Sun is warming you and you feel safe and deeply connected with Mother Earth. Now whisper gently three times:

Mother, Goddess, All of All of All, This is your loving child's Primal Call. Give me my name from thee alone, The secret name by which I am known.

Now sit quietly and let whatever thoughts or images flow into your mind. When you are ready, thump the floor three times gently with your left hand and return to this world. Make the sign of the Pentacle over your body and close the magick circle. Your 'AGLA' bandage, crystal, incense ash and stub of candle should all be rolled together and kept in a secure box. This is your initiator charm and can be used in personal spellworking when you need a really strong bind with the Elements.

31. Love charm

You will need:

- ★ 1 unripe lemon
- ★ 1 red ribbon
- ★ dried cloves

Best time: Any time your love
life needs a boost!

What to do:

Take the lemon and first tie the red ribbon around it widthways. Knot it and then tie it around the lemon lengthways and knot again. Take the end of the ribbon and tie it into a loop. You should now have a cross shape on your lemon made of ribbon with a loop at the top to hang it up by. Now fill the lemon spaces left between the ribbon, with the cloves. Stick them into the lemon skin until it is absolutely covered with cloves and only the red ribbon is showing.

Hang this charm above your bed or give it to a loved one. As it hangs there, the charm slowly pours out love power into your life until eventually, after quite a long time, the lemon will be completely dried up and then it must be taken down and buried in the earth.

32. To scry if your lover is faithful

You will need:

* ★ a crystal ball
* ★ a wooden or ceramic bowl
* ★ water
* ★ 1 fresh red chilli
* ★ 1 handful of cumin seeds
* ★ 1 pin

Best times: Preferably on the night of the Dark Moon, the New Moon or the Full Moon

What to do:

Place the crystal ball in the bowl and fill it with water until just covering the top of the crystal ball. Take the chilli and prick your lover's name in it with the pin. Look up at the Moon and throw the chilli into the bowl while calling your lover's name.

Now take the handful of cumin seeds and blow on them. Again, look up at the Moon and this time call your own name while throwing them into the water.

Now look into and through the crystal ball, letting your eyes relax and wander. If you can see the chilli surrounded or next to the cumin seeds, the auguries are good. If the chilli is quite separate from the cumin seeds the situation suggests a difficulty ahead.

 63. Party passion spell

You will need:

- ★ a charcoal burner or disposable charcoal barbecue
- ★ 4 red candles
- ★ a combination of any or all of the following – dried apple leaves, root ginger, rose petals, witch grass, caraway seeds and rosemary.

Best time:

Whenever your party needs a boost!

What to do:

(For this spell you should ideally scatter the powder over the hot burning coals outside. **Never** use a disposable barbecue inside the house. If you have a small indoor charcoal block or incense burner then it can be done inside.)

Firstly, grind up the herbs you are using in a pestle and mortar. Do not worry if they are a bit soggy as the ginger can create liquid. That's fine, but don't use too much ginger. Place the 4 red candles at each side of the burner and light them. Light also the charcoal burner or barbecue and wait for the coals to glow with heat. Sprinkle the powder over the coals saying three times over:

❧ *Love and lust and lust and love,*
  Tonight reach the heights of passion above.

34. A quick spell to look fabulous — first thing in the morning

You will need:

★ a full-length mirror
★ 1 ginseng root
★ a bowl of cold water

Best time:
First thing in the
morning!

What to do:

Stand in front of the full-length mirror if possible, completely naked with a big stretchy grin on your face and holding the ginseng root in your left hand. Look into your reflection in the mirror and, whatever part of your face or body you glance at, smile as wide as you can and think, 'How fabulous I look.' Keep the smile as you breath gently, deeply and calmly, all the time still thinking about how fabulous you are. When ready, say:

Diana, Astarte, Beauty Divine,
Bring a fabulous look to this body of mine.

Do this for about 10 minutes and then go and throw the ginseng root into the bowl of water and then splash your face with the energized cold water. When you have finished this ritual, take the ginseng root out of the water and bury it in earth, pouring the water over the top.

35. Seduction menu

You will need:

Main course

- ★ 1 avocado – sliced
- ★ 2 large tomatoes – sliced
- ★ 1 handful chopped parsley
- ★ 1 tbsp olive oil
- ★ 1 block of mozzarella cheese – diced
- ★ a small sprinkle of black pepper
- ★ ½ lemon – squeezed
- ★ warm garlic butter pitta bread

Dessert

- ★ 1 tub of vanilla ice cream
- ★ 1 punnet of fresh strawberries
- ★ 2 tbsp caster (superfine) sugar
- ★ a fresh cherry
- ★ ¼ pint (150 ml) double (heavy) cream

Drinks

- ★ Bloody Mary for the main course and pink champagne for the dessert

Ambience
- ★ violet scented and violet coloured candles
- ★ lavender perfume and lavender underwear

Best times: Full or Waxing Moon and when you want to get your lover!

What to do:
Light the candles, wear the underwear and put a modest amount of lavender-scented perfume on your pulse points (wrists, back of knees, neck). Now mix together the food ingredients of the main course into a salad and serve with warm garlic butter pitta bread and Bloody Mary. Follow with the ice cream, surrounded by strawberries, then covered with sugar and cream with a cherry on the top. Serve with pink champagne. (The combination of specific smells, colours, and tastes should be enough to get your lover seduced in a second!)

36. To recapture your youth

You will need:

★ 1 young shoot of bracken or fern
★ a flattering youthful photo of yourself
★ a square of green cloth
★ some white cotton
★ myrtle tea
★ aniseed or sweet cumin

Best time:

As soon as possible!

What to do:

Select your nicest, most youthful photo and place it on top of the green square of material. Place the young bracken shoot on top, gather up the folds of the cloth and tie securely with the white cotton. Keep the package somewhere cool and dark, such as buried in your garden or in the back of the freezer and forget it.

Drink a cup of warm myrtle tea on the first day of every consecutive 9 days (three times each month). That means each month on day 1, day 10 and day 19. On those particular days, take a bath with the sweet cumin or aniseed in it before midday.

37. Successful attraction in a job interview

Amongst the very many good herbs around, there are three secret herbs that are particularly known to be of benefit to those seeking a successful attraction at a job interview. However, they are hard to come by and if you do manage to find at least one of the three, treasure it well and carry it around with you, particularly when going for an interview.

The three herbs are:

★ yerw (yarrow)
★ wintera (winters bark)
★ spindle tree (wahoo) *this one is poisonous so handle with care*

Any one of these three herbs if carried in your pocket at a job interview should increase your chance of attraction success. (Unless of course someone else is carrying one of these herbs too! Then it would depend on whose piece is the most potent!)

38. To attract money to you

You will need:

* ★ 1 blue iris flower
* ★ a square of green cloth
* ★ some white cotton
* ★ a silver coin

Best time:

Whenever you are short of cash!

What to do:

Ask permission from the flower if removing from the ground, or buy already cut flowers, and then take the head of the blue iris flower and wrap it with a silver coin in a piece of green material tied up with the white cotton. Put it in your purse, pocket or bag and forget all about it. Money surprises should be attracted to you whenever it is carried upon your person.

39. For attraction and success in legal matters

You will need:

★ a piece of fresh ginger root
★ 1 pin
★ 1 orange ribbon

Best time: Any time

What to do:

Take a piece of fresh ginger root and prick it nine times with a pin. Put the pin carefully away and now bite a tiny piece of the ginger and chew it. Immediately take whatever legal documents you have that you need success with and blow on them quite hard. Now wrap an orange ribbon around the ginger root and keep it in your pocket for the day. Afterwards, bury it in the earth.

40. To remove a hex

You will need:

* ★ a thistle plant in a pot (optional)
* ★ equal parts of lemon juice and water
* ★ 1 pinch of red pepper
* ★ 1 purple candle

Best time:

If ever you feel someone may have hexed you and preferably in the light of a Full Moon

What to do:

Light the purple candle. Mix the lemon juice and water together in your cauldron. Add the pinch of red pepper and stir, saying:

*North, West, South and East,
Hex wane and all evil cease.
Purify me and safeguard my own,
Hex, be gone, only love fill my home.*

Now circle the candle over the top of the cauldron, widdershins, three times. Then blow out the candle with all your force, imagining the Hex being blown out at the same time. Now take the cauldron and sprinkle a little of the liquid at the north-facing end of the house. Walk to the west-facing end of the house and sprinkle a little more, walk to the south-facing end of the house and sprinkle a little more and then walk to the east-facing end of the house and sprinkle a little more.

Walk back to the north-facing end of the house and raise your arms above your head, saying very loudly, 'It is done,' and clap your hands once. The rest of the liquid in the cauldron can be emptied outside.

If you have a thistle plant, place it to one side, either on your doorstep or just outside your front door. The thistle plant is a very powerful Hex-breaking energizer. It also protects from negativity and ill-doers and draws strength to its owner.

41. For sexy dreams

Many people have heard how good eating cheese is for inducing dreams at night, but there are ways to add certain herbs and foods that can direct the way your dreams go!

You will need:

★ a piece of strong cheddar cheese
★ a glass of cider
★ dried violets or violet oil
★ fresh rosemary
★ a piece of pink quartz
★ 1 ginseng root

Best time: Just before bed

What to do:

Just before going to bed, eat a small repast
of strong cheddar cheese and a glass of
cider. Place some dried violets or violet
oil, and some rosemary under your pillow
and get into bed holding a pink quartz
crystal in your left hand and a ginseng
root in your right hand. As you drift off to
sleep, think of the one you love and you
may well be amazed at the power of your
thoughts!

42. To reignite a fading passion

If the new hairstyle, facelift or diet hasn't worked, there's only one thing for it – a reignite spell.

You will need:

★ 1 handful of dried milk
★ lavender oil
★ 1 sachet of dried lavender
★ 1 white daisy
★ something white to wear

What to do:

In the bathroom, light a pink candle and take a purifying bath of warm water mixed with a handful of dried milk and lavender oil. Whilst in the bath, look into the candle flame and pray to Venus-Isis for Her support. The words should be your own and come from the heart. Perhaps finishing your prayer with something like:

Venus-Isis, mote it be,
Bless this spell with love for me,
Amen.

Now place under the bed a sachet of dried lavender and a fresh white daisy. Wear something white to bed. It may not happen immediately, but if you can relax and put the spell out of your mind once these rituals have been performed, you should soon have the passion reignited. It is very rare for Venus-Isis to ignore a call from one of her daughters!

43. Love magick suggestions for a handfasting

For the Woman:

Wear a white robe with a headdress of ivy and daisies and a silver ring.

For the Man:

Wear a white robe with a headdress of holly and oak leaves and a gold ring.

Ambience:

Rose oil in burners, lavender incense and plenty of sparklers!

Loving Cup:

Elderflower cordial, champagne and sparkling water mixed together with sliced strawberries and tiny flecks of edible gold leaf floating on the surface.

Frosted Grapes:

Dip red grapes in egg white and then caster (superfine) sugar and leave to set and frost in the refrigerator.

Chocolate Roses:

Take tiny rose leaves, wash and dip them in hot melted chocolate on one side. Leave them to harden in the refrigerator and then gently peel the rose leaves away from the chocolate. Serve the chocolate leaves with the frosted grapes.

Ginger Joy Cake:

Take two packets of ginger biscuits (cookies) and soak them in sherry until the biscuits are slightly soft. Pack the biscuits (cookies) lengthways in two rows, sandwiched with double (whipping) cream between each biscuit. Now cover the whole block with double (whipping) cream and sprinkle grated chocolate over the top. Leave in the refrigerator to set. Serve with strawberries, raspberries and cream, sprinkled with a little grated fresh nutmeg, caster sugar and mint leaves.

44. To bring love into your life

Either go to one of the many sacred pools situated around the countryside or find your own water feature and make it your own sacred place, returning whenever you feel like it. Take a metal offering and, if possible, break it in two pieces, throwing one into the water and keeping the other on your person. If you can't break the object in two, then try and twist or fold it instead. If that is not possible, buy a pair of earrings and throw one in and keep the other. Stand facing the water and lift up both your arms to the skies and say three times:

> *Blessed Goddess, the One,*
> *Accept this gift from your daughter,*
> *Let love fill my world and*
> *Let love flood this water.*

Now take a small amount of the sacred love water back home with you and keep it on your altar or in a special place. Use it in your love spells or just let it slowly evaporate over time into the Ether around you.

45. Passion potion

This is a great drink for you and your loved one to share on a special night of lurve!

You will need:

- ★ 1 bottle of red wine
- ★ 1 sprig of lemon balm
- ★ 1 bay leaf
- ★ 5 blackberries
- ★ 5 capers
- ★ 5 cardamom seeds
- ★ 3 tablespoons of caster (superfine) sugar
- ★ 1 red candle

Best time:
When you are in the mood for love!

What to do:
In your cauldron pour a bottle of red wine.
Add a sprig of lemon balm, 1 bay leaf, 5
blackberries, 5 capers, 5 cardamom seeds
and 3 tablespoons of caster sugar. Heat very
gently and allow the flavours to infuse.
Drain through muslin into a glass bowl. (If
you have a red glass bowl – even better.)
Light a red candle and share the drink
between yourselves, toasting the magick of
passion each time you take a sip, saying:

Blessed be, Planet Mars
All hail, to the stars
This night, love is ours.

46. For success on a first date

You will need:

★ a piece of white paper
★ red ink
★ 1 stalk of yarrow
★ a piece of red cotton
  (or red ribbon)
★ musk incense

Best time:
Four days before
your date

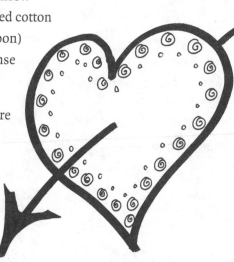

What to do:

At your altar, take a piece of white paper and write in red the name of your loved one plus your name. Place a stalk of yarrow in the middle and tie the paper up into a packet with red cotton or ribbon. Now burn a stick of musk incense and waft the packet through the smoke, chanting:

 Strength of the Ether,
Inflamed in me,
Bring my love to (name)
Who in time I shall see,
Yarrow burn with love's bright flame,
The power is mine in first love's name.

Now kiss the packet twice and then hide it somewhere carefully where no one will find it. After three nights have passed, bury the packet in earth.

47. To scry information on the one you fancy

You will need:

★ white or purple candles
★ sandalwood incense
★ beetroot juice
★ oil of frankincense

Best times: Dark Moon,
New Moon, Full Moon

What to do:

Do this preferably in a darkened room, lit only by white or purple candles. Burn some sandalwood incense. Take your cauldron and fill it with fresh spring water if possible. Take some beetroot juice and drip 3 drops from a great height into the cauldron. Now blow three times on the surface of the liquid and call the name of your loved one.

Take some oil of frankincense and drip 3 drops from a great height into the cauldron. Now blow again three times on the surface of the liquid and whisper your own name.

Look into the cauldron at the patterns emerging and see what relevance they have concerning this person. You can repeat the exercise twice more using the same cauldron to look further, but after three goes, the water must be returned to the earth.

48. To be a Love Goddess for the night!

You will need:

- ★ 6 jasmine-scented candles
- ★ 1 handful of dried milk powder
- ★ 1 handful of crushed rose petals
- ★ ylang ylang oil
- ★ something pink to wear
- ★ 1 pink candle

Best time:
Whenever you want to!

What to do:

In your bathroom light 6 candles scented with jasmine. Take a warm bath and add a handful of dried milk powder, a handful of crushed rose petals and 3 drops of ylang ylang oil essence.

After your bath, change into something pink and then go to your altar. Light a pink candle and raise your arms skywards. Intone:

I am a daughter of the Goddess
  The Goddess is love
  I am a daughter of love
  I am a Love Goddess
  Grow now, O love,
  Descend, O love.
  Love, bring the love to me. Amen.

Extinguish the candle carefully and enjoy your Love Goddess powers!

49. To add a little magickal zest into your evening!

You will need:

★ 1 cotton wool pad
★ geranium oil
★ 1 thin white cotton handkerchief

Best time: After 12 noon

What to do:

Take a cotton wool pad and place 2 drops of neat geranium oil on it. Wrap the pad within a thin white cotton handkerchief. Carry it in your pocket or bag when you are going out.

Place the handkerchief discreetly on the table when you have arrived at your destination and leave it there for the course of the evening.

50. To discourage an admirer

If all else fails and you are suffering from the attentions of an unwanted admirer, try carrying a piece of chicory on you whenever you are in their presence. Also, sprinkle a little dried coconut in their footsteps after they have left.

51. To find out if your lover is serious about you

This is a very old spell and can be adapted to find out other information, using the ingredients. However, here is the basic spell for love information.

You will need:
★ rice paper
★ red food colouring
★ bread dough

Best times:
Dark Moon, New Moon, Full Moon

What to do:
Take some rice paper and cut it into five small, identical circles. Using the red food colouring, write 'Yes' on one circle, then 'No' on another circle, then 'Maybe' on another circle. Leave the final two circles blank.

Now make or buy some bread dough and carefully place each rice-paper circle in its own bread dough covering, rolling it, so you end up with five balls of dough – each one containing an individual rice paper circle in the middle. Make sure the dough completely covers the rice paper.

Now bake the dough balls in the oven, then take out and leave to cool.

Pick one dough ball at random and throw it away without looking at it – this is called a 'donation'.

With the final four balls in front of you, ask the question, '*Is my lover true to me?*' and then start opening the dough balls one by one to find an answer. The first dough ball that has something written inside is your main answer and the others answer any further questions you might have. If any of the dough balls are blank it means nothing is definite at this stage.

52. To find out if a love affair will be successful

You will need:

★ rose incense
★ 1 pink candle
★ 1 pin
★ 1 dried bay leaf

Best time: Midnight

What to do:

Firstly, light an incense stick or cone scented with rose. Then take a pink candle and write the name of your loved one down one side of the candle with a pin. Light the candle. Take your cauldron and fill it with fresh water. Crush a dried bay leaf in your hands and throw it into the water, saying:

Aporrheta, secrets reveal to me
Hidden Arcanum that I may see
How my true love's thinking of me.

When the wax begins to melt, hold the candle over the cauldron and drip 9 drops of wax into the water. Return the candle to its setting and look into the cauldron for any images or messages relating to your love affair.

53. To enchant a gift for your lover

When you next give your lover a gift, whatever it may be (as long as it's not too big – like a sofa or something!), a nice thing to do is to enchant the item with good fortune and happiness (this works particularly well on jewellery).

You will need:

★ a small dish of earth
★ a small glass of water
★ 1 red candle
★ sandalwood incense
★ a small dish of salt

Best time:

One day before giving the gift

What to do:

Go to your altar and arrange in a row: a small dish of earth, a small glass of water, a red candle, a cone or stick of sandalwood incense and a small dish of salt. Now take the item and sprinkle some earth over it, saying:

Auriel, I invoke thee to protect this (name of gift).

Then sprinkle a little water over it, saying:

Gabriel, I invoke thee to protect this (name of gift).

Then pass it **over** the flame of the candle, saying:

Michael, I invoke thee to protect this (name of gift).

Then pass it through the smoke of the incense, saying:

Raphael, I invoke thee to protect this (name of gift).

Finally, sprinkle some salt over it, saying:

Spirit of the Moon, I invoke thee to ask for your blessing on this (name of gift), in the name of love and the All of All of All. So mote it be. Amen.

(At this point you may need to take a soft cloth and clean the item gently in case of any residue.)

Now your gift is enchanted and ready to be passed on to a loved one.

54. A spell to choose between two (or more!) lovers

If you really want to know, do this spell!

You will need:
- ★ dried butter beans (or similar dried beans)
- ★ 1 purple candle

Best time:
Waning Moon

What to do:

However many lovers you may have, choose the same amount of dried butter beans. Write the names or initials of your lovers on the beans (one to each bean) and put the beans in your cauldron.

Light a purple candle. Sit quietly and think of the different people and then pick up the cauldron and gently sway it widdershins three times. Replace the cauldron without looking inside and say loudly, 'Flow!' Still not looking into the cauldron, remove one of the two beans (or a handful if there are many!) and cast it (or them) behind you, again without looking. Keep doing this until you only have one bean left in the cauldron.

Relax your mind and try and think who it is or who you would like it to be. When ready, say loudly, 'So!' and take out the last bean. There is the name of your chosen one.

 55. An amulet to attract love

You will need:

- ★ 1 stone
- ★ 1 pink candle
- ★ a glass of cider
- ★ musk oil

Best time:

Night of a New Moon

What to do:

Before starting the spell you must first find yourself a 'lucky' stone. How or where you find it doesn't matter as long as it's special to you. It can be picked up from a beach or a wood or even bought in a shop. It's up to you.

Now bring it to your altar, light a pink candle and drip one drop of the wax onto the stone, saying, 'Abraxas.' Taking a pin, carefully write in the wax droplet the number '365'. Then leave the whole thing to soak overnight in a small glass containing cider and one drop of musk oil.

The following morning, remove the stone and wash it under running water. Don't worry if the wax falls off because the magick symbols have been infused within the stone overnight. Place the stone in your pocket for attraction power.

56. A time spell to attract someone special

This spell must be done at the seaside and cannot be reproduced within the home because of the importance of the tidal waves of the Sea.

Go to the edge of the Sea and write the name of that someone special in the sand. Now sit and count how many waves it takes before the name is washed away. The number of waves is the same number of attempts you have to try and attract that someone special before your luck runs out.

57. Mistletoe merriment

The evergreen mistletoe is a very magickal plant and kissing under the mistletoe is well known for its romantic associations, especially at Yule.

Hanging bunches of mistletoe in your house promotes health, happiness and love.

Cut at Midsummer's day, mistletoe is particularly potent in magickal abilities; the other best time to cut mistletoe is on the sixth day of the Moon.

Mistletoe growing in an oak tree was especially rare. If Druids found it, they would cut it down with a gold knife and catch it in a white cloth or cloak so it would not fall and touch the Earth. Anything that grew in an oak tree was believed to have been sent from the heavens above.

Putting a sprig of mistletoe under your pillow before sleeping will bring dreams of love. Putting a sprig under your loved one's pillow should make them dream of you!

58. One enchanted evening

In the month of May, sit with your loved one under a New Moon and share an orange together. Gather up any pips and take them home. Rinse under warm water and immediately plant them in the Earth – either in your garden or in a pot on the windowsill. If a plant grows, a marriage may well be on its way!

59. Fairy fortune

If you are lucky enough to find a fairy ring (a ring of mushrooms or a ring of daisies or a ring of grass that is growing out of kilter with the surrounding grass) then this is the spell for you! Simply skip around the ring six times – widdershins if you are female, deosil if you are male. Then sit down outside the fairy ring and make a wish. Within 6 days you will either meet the person who is to become your next lover or your wish will come true!

60. For steamy success at a party!

Before going out to a party, wear under your clothes a pink garter with a rosebud tucked into it. Make sure no one knows you are wearing these items and then just before leaving the party, secretly drop the garter and rose bud on the floor – making sure no one sees you doing it! Now wait to see if anyone picks them up.

If the rosebud only is picked up: you've found a winner!
If the garter only is picked up: best let it go!
If both items are picked up: you have the best of both worlds!
If neither of the items are picked up: there's obviously no one there good enough for you!

Of course, what you do after that is entirely up to you!

How to Party – Practice & Rituals!

Now you've practised The Look and you look great, you've practised The Attitude and you're In the Know, you've practised a few spells and you've got it figured, what better gift than knowing How to Party?! Here it is, the real thing – you're putting your steps into real practice with a party attitude wherever you go!

How to Party means knowing how to use your particular talents in spellworking and rituals as well as having a great time! Here are a few basic rituals that any well-trained Witch will know about – and if she doesn't, she had better learn about them fast if she's *really* going to party!

 Drawing Down the Moon

This is a very well known title in witchy circles for essentially 'becoming the Goddess temporarily' in order to add power to your spellworking. Sometimes spells take quite a while to get going or deliver their magick and sometimes it only takes a couple of hours – however, if you are in need of an immediate response, Drawing Down the Moon should help you get it. It's particularly useful when scrying. When you are safely within your magick circle, having welcomed the Elements and whatever spirits or guides you work with, you then acknowledge the Goddess Herself and draw Her essential spirit down into the circle and into you. Whilst you are in that frame, your spellworking will be enhanced by Her immediate power, which touches and envelopes yours. This is the method most commonly used amongst my witchy friends.

You will need:

- ★ a small chalice of elderflower wine
- ★ a small china dish of cupcakes or similar
- ★ a small china bowl of sea salt crystals
- ★ a small glass goblet of water
- ★ a small china bowl of altar oil
- ★ 1 white candle
- ★ 1 red candle
- ★ 1 black candle

First, light the three candles and then stand within the magick circle, in front of the altar and using your magick wand, draw the symbol of the Hey in the air above the altar – the gateway between the two worlds. Draw it three times, from left to right, right to left and upright. Place the middle finger of your left hand into the bowl of anointing oil and make the sign of the Goddess (a circle, with a semicircle on top) on your forehead, in the region of your third eye. Then, holding your athame in your left hand and your magick wand in your right hand, raise both hands high and recite a welcoming chant (the following is one taken from the Akashic Library and one that I often use myself):

> I call to you, Great Goddess
> For to me is given the Truth
>   of the Soul
> I am now the Three in One
>   Maid, Mother and Crone
> I am the Earth, the Moon
>   and the Water
> I am the Spirit, the Light
>   and the Matter
> I call to you, Great Goddess
> For I am now the One
> Draw down into me and live
> For we are one
>   together and always.

Take the athame and dip it into the bowl of salt, saying:

❦ I consecrate this salt in the name of the Goddess,
so mote it be. ❧

Take the athame and dip it into the goblet of
water, saying:

❦ I consecrate this water in the name of the Goddess,
so mote it be. ❧

Take the athame and dip it into the chalice of
wine, saying:

❦ I consecrate this wine in the name of the
Goddess, so mote it be. ❧

Take the athame and place it on
top of the cake, saying:

❦ I consecrate this cake in the
name of the Goddess, so mote it
be. ❧

Now using the athame, put 3 dashes of salt into the goblet of water and stir widdershins. Next pour some of the wine and take a piece of cake and put them both in the cauldron, then sprinkle a little of the salted water over the top – this is your offering to the Goddess. Take the cauldron and pass it through the flames of the three Goddess candles. Then eat the remainder of the cake and wine at your leisure, within the circle.

When you have finished, dip the middle finger on your left hand again into the anointing oil and make the sign of the protective Pentacle over your body, by touching your left hip, then your third eye area, then your right hip, then your left shoulder, then your right shoulder, and then back down to your left hip again. At this moment you are fully empowered by the Goddess and can proceed with spellworking or any other work you have to do, within the magick circle. The salted water has now been energized and can also be used for protective spellworking. Whatever spells or rituals you do next, remember to use the three Goddess candles if passing anything through flame.

When all ritual and procedures
are finished, empty the cauldron
into a pot of earth, and say:

⬥ *With good despatch, joyful
despatch,
Blessed Mother, guide my way.
All fairies, angels and spirits
Return through the power of the
Hey.
Goddess touched – all love to thee,
As I will – so mote it be,
Amen.*

Close the Hey with your magick
wand by repeating the three
opening movements in the
opposite direction and closing
the circle.

Pyramid or Cone of Power

This is another word for the magickal energy that is produced, usually within a circle, when you are spellworking. One of the reasons you work within a magick circle (apart from protection) is so that the boundaries of the circle can contain the power that you build. If you work without a circle, the power wafts away as you work, because there is nothing to hold it around you. So the circle acts rather like a bowl or bag, which holds your treasure!

The reason it is called a Pyramid or Cone of Power is because essentially the energy that you call forth either pours from your self, spiralling upwards as you contact the Ether, and widens out into a pyramid or cone shape (or pours down from the Ether spiralling towards you, according to your needs and abilities). Although the power has no one definite colour, it can be seen quite well, depending on the strength of your workings. Usually it is like a translucent ripple or haze in the air. This can change to a misty white fog, a pale-ish blue fog, or a golden shine depending on what you are doing and how well you are doing it! Practice makes perfect!

As you concentrate on ritual, chanting, words, symbols, dance and so forth, you give off a recognized signature that reaches out to the Ethereal Plane and connects the forces to you through the spiralling pyramid or cone. By chanting, dancing and singing, you slowly raise the energy levels within your circle. You may find that the chanting and singing gets louder and the dancing gets more energetic as you soak up the energy and give off your own magickal energy force. The whole movement reaches a crescendo and then stops and it is at this moment of stoppage that the power is there, to be used in your work. The only way to explain it is that the more you practise, the more you will be able to 'feel' a response and notice how much more intense the surroundings become. And that is *your* power to use in *your* spellworking.

A

Making Your Own Poppet

Poppet is a figurine that Witches use in various ways by animating it on the Ethereal Plane and doing sympathetic magick with it. This is the original 'wax doll' that most people think is for negative purposes – the truth is, of course, completely different!

The best way to start off with Poppets is by making one of yourself! Once you're in the groove with your own Poppet, you might then like to carry on by making Poppets for others to use with healing spells and helpful spells on their behalf, when requested to do so. The idea behind making a Poppet is to fashion it in such a way that it resembles the person it represents. In this instance, if you are making it for yourself, it must be identifiably male or female depending on your gender and although the original Poppets were made from wax, you can actually use anything, such as a plastic figurine, a wooden sculpture, melted candles, or even paper!

First, fashion a naked doll and then 'dress it' with your own gear. If you can, take a cutting of your own hair and glue it to the head,

take a nail clipping and glue it to the hands or feet and then dress it in fabric from something you wear – cut out a bit of an upturned hem or similar! In Bulgaria and other European countries, I have met Witches who say that you should make the sign of the Pentacle on the naked doll in your own saliva before dressing it. Other Witches suggest incorporating raw egg, Gem Elixirs, and so on, within the body to give the Poppet a 'living substance' to connect the animation with the Ether. It is totally up to you and what feels right for you – after all, YOU are the Witch here. Fashion the Poppet to resemble yourself as much as possible. If you have freckles, birth-marks or even tattoos – put them on your Poppet!

Once the Poppet is ready, take it to the altar or table and bless it in your own special way – through the Elements and through the love of the Goddess. While it is being blessed, you can incorporate naming it with your secret name and the power that you need. So, for example, if you have money problems, you could fashion a tiny cheque or purse and hang it on your Poppet and call forth financial aid. If you have a health problem, you could 'heal' the area on your Poppet with potions and bandages or whatever is applicable, and call forth healing power, and so on. As a Sexy Sorceress, of course, your Poppet should look as gorgeous as you can possibly make it and then, in time, those attributes will be transferred to you through the power of sympathetic magick. This Poppet is a 'little you' and all that you do with it should be reflected in your life through the sympathetic magick being applied. The possibilities are endless and, having endowed your Poppet with success, you should find that you are directing your life in a very positive and successful way.

Offerings and Gift Giving

It is always a good idea to give some offering to the Goddess, God, Elements or Spirits that you are in contact with as you spellwork. Most Ethereals have particular colours and items that are special to them and it is one of your responsibilities as a good Witch to find out what they are. Basic offerings, however, are chocolate, gems, wine, tobacco, cakes, flowers, milk and water. If you have some item special to you and want to enchant it, you can break it in half and offer one half to the Goddess or to whichever Entity you are contacting and keep the other half on your person. This ensures a link between you and the Etheric World and is a very special talisman. After ritually offering the half-portion of the gift, always bury the Entity's half in the earth or throw it in running water. This ensures it is delivered to them on the Ethereal Plane. Another good way of making an offering is by burning it in a candle. (However, obviously items like chocolate would not be particularly good for this one!) Anything made of paper is ideal but do make sure you have an extinguisher or bowl of water handy in case of mishaps.

Sending a Spell through the Ether

I spend a lot of my time visiting different planes in the Ether and am constantly being amazed by its ever-changing substance and the continual learning experiences I have there. To explain a little of what I have learned, and to describe the Ether to you, I can say that I believe the Ether to be composed mainly of five elemental astral forces, which are: Moon Spirit, which relates to magnetism; Sun Fire, which relates to light particles; Earth Matter, which relates to calories; Wind Air, which relates to electricity; and Sea Water; which relates to sound waves.

When you send a spell you can choose with which elemental forces you would like to work. The more you understand about these forces, the more relevant they will become to your individual spells and the more easily they will work for you. The four basic ways of sending spells (that you probably know already) are: burning through a candle flame (Fire); wafting through an incense stick (Air); burying in the ground (Earth); or dropping in rivers (Water). However, if you increase your knowledge of the astral forces – magnetism, light, calories, electricity and sound waves – you can then send spells through the power of auric magnets, scrying, dance and movements, brain wave projections and singing chants. You can also send spells through personally wearing, using, eating or drinking them (as long as they are not poisonous, obviously!) and so on.

The more you investigate, the more you will discover where your talents prefer to work. Basically, though, the idea is to send a spell through the Ether to the spirit world, to the Goddess, the God, Angels and Fairies, so that together you can effect the magick that you need and change the physical world with the power of the ethereal world. Whenever you are in contact with magickal forces, you are in the Ether. So if you happen to have an amazing talent for Scrying, but haven't managed to perfect Astral Travel yet – chill! You're still contacting the Ether, you're just doing it in your special way – is all! Dreams are probably the easiest way to get in tune with the Ether and once you become aware of the quirky nature of the Ether's movements, you will probably find yourself recognizing its signature in many more things that you do!

Making the Sigil of the Pentacle

This is used a lot as a powerful protection sigil and one that connects with the Ether. It can be made in different ways, to invoke, to banish, to connect with particular energies, and so on. However, the very first way of making the sigil upon yourself, which I feel is important to learn, is the following:

Stand upright and with your right arm extended, sweep it down towards the left hip area. Now bring it straight up above your head and then down to the right hip area. Now bring it up across the body to your left shoulder area and then straight across (although you will find it making an arc since you should not bend the arm as you are doing the sweep) to your right shoulder area, and then back down to the left hip. Do not bend your elbows, keep your arm straight and do this sigil in one fluid movement. You can do this sigil at any time and whenever you feel the need of protection or extra concentration. You can finish the Pentacle by sweeping your arm in a circular movement, widdershins or deosil from the final point at the left hip, around the body and back to the left hip.

♥ Inviting Spirits to Join You

The spirits are all around you, protecting you, loving you and caring for you. Sometimes, for example at Samhain, it is lovely to make an invitation to the spirits to join you for a party or if you particularly want to get in touch with someone. There is always the possibility of mischievous spirits joining in, but these are not essentially bad spirits, simply child-like ones that enjoy havoc (rather like naughty younger brothers and sisters if you like). If this happens, you simply send them firmly and kindly back to where they came from by telling them to go and making the Pentacle sigil with your magick wand or athame.

At Samhain, it is nice to set an extra place at the table for your spirit guests and leave them gifts of chocolate, tobacco and silver coins. A black candle is best for contacting spirits because the black colour represents the Crone Entity of the Goddess, who regularly walks with spirits. Pumpkin candles are used to light the way for the spirits to join you, but if you are contacting them at times other than Samhain, then normal lanterns or candles placed in a 'pathway' within your circle do the trick. A circle of light is also a nice way to illuminate your magick space and has the added advantage of protection. You can physically make the circle of light with candles around your space. Alternatively, using your athame, start from the east, widdershins, and point it to the floor, visualizing golden flames of light streaming from the end of your athame. Then slowly turn widdershins within your circle, keeping the athame pointing outwards and downwards, streaming light as it goes until you return to the starting point.

Finally, as far as having fun goes and as in all party celebrations (it makes no difference whether you're at a swish social event, the local bar, a school dance or even the back seat of a car!) – you are a Sexy Sorceress and you *know* how to party! With every party of course comes the possible downside, so be sure to have preparations for that and you can't go wrong. Back again in my grandmother's day it was the bus fare home, so if things got out of hand you could make your excuses and hop on a bus! Now, it's more like a confirmed ride home or a cab fare – but if you've got it arranged *before* you party, then you have an escape route if you tire of the fun! After all, everyone knows what it feels like to try and phone a cab when you're three sheets to the wind: not a nice experience and one that you easily give up on – leading to disasters, usually! So get it sorted before you party then you're safe to really let rip!

Try to pace yourself too – because a drunken Sexy Sorceress can muddle her spells quite easily and end up with Mr Havoc instead of Mr Gorgeous! If you find your elixirs and potions are going down too fast, off you go to the safety of the bathroom! Not only is the mirror there, but water too, so you can splash your face, drink some water and fix your make-up. And if the very worst happens, you can always invisibly escape from the bathroom to the safety of your cab home (aren't bathrooms great places!) Another couple of tricks to remember are those old sayings: 'Less is more' and 'When in doubt – don't'. These two can apply to almost anything – think about it! And finally, do remember, Tiger – there is ALWAYS, always, another party around the corner!

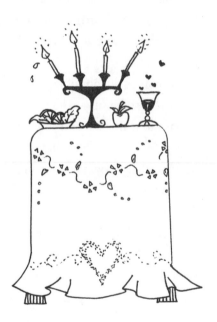

Essential Shopping!

Sexy Sorceresses are simply great at shopping! They know instinctively what they need and what is useful to have at the bottom of their bag or hidden in their shoe for emergencies! These are some of the essentials that every Sexy Sorceress should have or have access to!

For a Successful Look

★ sunglasses
★ make-up
★ false hair
★ hairspray
★ stick-on glittery stuff
★ scarves – lots of them
★ cigarette holder or something to chew on
★ lipstick and mascara
★ mints
★ a fan to flutter behind
★ a hankie – Granny knows best!

Finally, I would say **the most important thing for a successful Look is confidence!** Keep a bag full of confidence with you at all times and you will always be the centre of attention.

 # For a Perfect Know How

★ perfume
★ cab card
★ diary and pen
★ small notebook for writing phone numbers down
★ confident stride or sexy squirm
★ squeezy lemon (for repelling would-be attackers!)
★ mobile phone
★ a big smile!

And **for the perfect Know How**, you've guessed it; **courage is what you need**. Keep a bag full of courage with you and people will flock to your side wanting a bit of your know how!

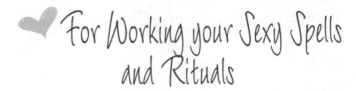

For Working your Sexy Spells and Rituals

- ★ athame
- ★ magick wand
- ★ cauldron
- ★ mirror
- ★ crystal ball
- ★ earth
- ★ water
- ★ incense
- ★ candles

- ★ herbs
- ★ oils
- ★ ribbons
- ★ coloured paper
- ★ sticks
- ★ stones
- ★ leaves
- ★ flowers
- ★ grasses

- ★ pine cones
- ★ elderflower cordial or wine
- ★ cake
- ★ chocolate!

And **the ultimate thing you'll need here?** Yep – **communication!** If you have a bag full of communication at your finger tips – nothing can stop you communicating your Sexy Spells and Rituals.

For When You Want to Party

★ condoms (obviously!)

★ money – for emergencies such as cabs home, last minute cigarettes, or to tip the waiter!

★ matches or a lighter – for candles, lighting your cigarettes, or singeing anyone who becomes too excited over you!

★ a squeezy plastic lemon or rape alert claxon – just in case you need to call for back up or stop someone in their tracks!

★ headache pills – the last thing you want is a headache!

★ small bottle of water – to take your headache pills with, or to wash away tear-smudged mascara or even to sip from time to time

★ hankies, tissues or toilet paper – see above, and also to dab your nose with if necessary! No Sexy Sorceress EVER sniffs!

★ a pen – to write your lover's phone number!

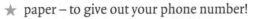

- ★ paper – to give out your phone number!
- ★ lipstick and mirror – if you have no other make-up, your lips are where the concentration comes from and is also going to, so you'll need a mirror to see what you're doing!
- ★ spare pair of stockings – very useful – for tying broken fan belts in cars, straining the sodden potato chips out of your beer, changing into if you get a hole in your original pair, keeping your trousers up or party games!
- ★ mobile phone – excellent for quick exits!
- ★ Chanel No 5 – the most powerful perfume for attraction!
- ★ mints – a quick refresher before the kissing starts!
- ★ sunglasses – to lurk behind and encourage exploration!
- ★ a tiny book (such as this one!) – to hide inside and be tempted out of!

For Rest and Rejuvenation!

- ★ cucumbers
- ★ teabags
- ★ wind chimes
- ★ dreamcatchers
- ★ music
- ★ a cat
- ★ pillows
- ★ home-made vegetable soup
- ★ baths
- ★ more baths
- ★ candles
- ★ scents
- ★ fresh air
- ★ deep breathing
- ★ yoga
- ★ meditation
- ★ picnics
- ★ laughter
- ★ sleep!

With all this excitement going on, it is quite usual for a Sexy Sorceress to forget to sleep! Don't go there, for goodness' sake. If you don't sleep, you can't rejuvenate and if you don't rejuvenate, your powers may start to wane. So take heed – party on, Sister, by all means, but when you feel the need to crash, stuff the excitement and find a cool place to lay your head and rejuvenate. Even though you may be the most exciting Witch that ever flew, you *will* need time-out for yourself. So sleep for a while and let the fairies guard you with their wings.

Final Word

To sum up this book, an easy statement would be, 'The Goddess is love – you are the Goddess – therefore, you are love – that's about it, folks!' It doesn't matter by what name you call the Goddess, whether Isis, The Lady, Mother, Hecate, Spirit of the Moon or even the Feminine Principal. It doesn't matter whether you believe in male or female, in both, or in the Great Creator. The Goddess doesn't have only one particular title; She has them all – She is love, She is everything and She is everywhere.

The important point to remember and hold onto is that we are all part of the Goddess, and She is part of us. That may seem a pretty radical statement to accept since most of us have been exposed to a religion or dogma of one sort or another at some time in our lives. We are not taught to think of ourselves as **A ⋆ PART ⋆ OF ⋆ GOD** but more as **APART ⋆ OF ⋆ GOD**. This tends to indicate an inferior position rising to feelings of guilt, fear and sorrow, which in turn 'keeps us in our place' and 'under control'. However, truly, the Goddess does not want us to be burdened with these negative thoughts. After all, with the Goddess and us, rules don't exist – we just have to concentrate on keeping the love thing going. If we can all learn to tap into our spirituality, we are tapping into our own Goddess and then we are as we should be – whole. It's like an immediate help line or safety net.

People often say, 'If God is love then why does He allow terrible things to happen?' And what we are saying is that God (the Goddess) is in charge of everything and we are powerless to do anything ourselves (which when you think of it is an awful burden to put on anyone and simply not true). What do we mean, 'Why does God allow ...?' Why don't we ask ourselves, 'Why do *we* allow ...?' Yes, the Goddess is the Supreme Being, the One, but as we are all a part of the

Goddess in our human form, it is up to us to do our bit too. After all, we have the power within ourselves to make huge changes, not only in our own lives but in the lives of others, because we are all part of this great spiritual Ether. If we become aware of our powers and use them, we become more aware of the central Goddess figure and our lives dramatically improve. As humans we are all born with the same equipment, despite our geography or skin colour and we have to remember that the power comes from *within* us, not around us. Once we access that power, we are using our Goddess talents and can do pretty much anything!

So there you have it: Sexy Spells for a Sexy Sorceress! As you can see it will take commitment and practice – but if you persevere you can change your life and, oh wow, what a life it can be! You have accessed your soul and found a vibrant, wonderful person hiding within you – and, even better, you now have the power to do anything you want and all in the name of love! Remember, though, you're not only a star, you're a fully fledged, world-wide, Sexy Sorceress! By all means hold on to the kitten within, but *do* go prowling, Tiger, and, as always,

Blessed be!